John Kennedy

Old Testament criticism and the rights of the unlearned

Being a plea for the rights and powers of non-experts in the study of Holy

Scripture

John Kennedy

Old Testament criticism and the rights of the unlearned
Being a plea for the rights and powers of non-experts in the study of Holy Scripture

ISBN/EAN: 9783337283353

Printed in Europe, USA, Canada, Australia, Japan

Cover: Foto ©Lupo / pixelio.de

More available books at **www.hansebooks.com**

Present Day Primers

OLD TESTAMENT CRITICISM

AND

THE RIGHTS OF THE UNLEARNED

BEING A PLEA

FOR THE RIGHTS AND POWERS OF NON-EXPERTS

IN THE STUDY OF HOLY SCRIPTURE

BY THE

REV. JOHN KENNEDY, M.A., D.D.

HONORARY PROFESSOR, NEW COLLEGE, LONDON
AUTHOR OF 'THE SELF-REVELATION OF JESUS CHRIST'
'THE RESURRECTION OF JESUS CHRIST, AN HISTORICAL FACT'
ETC., ETC.

'In understanding be men.'—1 COR. xiv. 20

THE RELIGIOUS TRACT SOCIETY

56 PATERNOSTER ROW AND 65 ST. PAUL'S CHURCHYARD

1897

OLD TESTAMENT CRITICISM

AND

THE RIGHTS OF THE UNLEARNED

BY

REV. JOHN KENNEDY, M.A., D.D.

PREFACE

THE object of this book is to set forth the relative positions of the Learned and Unlearned in the study of Holy Scripture,—meaning by the unlearned that great class of students who, however intelligent, do not possess the advantage of personal acquaintance with the languages in which the Scripture was originally written, or who, even if they have acquired some acquaintance with these languages, are not competent to form a judgement on questions which depend exclusively or mainly on the niceties of pure scholarship. The rights and legitimate functions of this class, which with scant propriety we call the unlearned, need to be safeguarded. There is a disposition in many quarters to recognize a class of specialists among Bible students, analogous to the class of acknowledged specialists in the departments of theoretic and practical science, and even to allow them a more exclusive authority than is often allowed to these. Questions which are agitating

the public mind to its very depth, and which involve
the most serious issues, in relation to the integrity
and trustworthiness of what we have been accustomed
to regard as the Word of God, and in relation to
the highest spiritual interests, are declared to be
'emphatically not people's questions.' 'The solution
of these difficulties, if they are ever to be solved,'
we are told, 'can only be the work of men who are
equipped for the service with special philological and
historical knowledge and acumen.' And at the feet
of those who are so equipped, they who are not are
bidden to sit as humble learners till the solution is
published with authority.

In the following pages the writer endeavours to
separate truth from untruth in this matter, and
to maintain the legitimate rights of those who may
be called non-experts; and having done so, he sets
forth certain reasons which justify these non-experts
in holding by the main positions of the older
criticism of the Old Testament scriptures, and rejecting the main positions of the newer,—reasons
which are in no respect inconsistent with the highest
scholarship, and whose soundness no scholarship can
neutralize or render doubtful.

CONTENTS

---◆---

PART FIRST

PART SECOND

OLD TESTAMENT CRITICISM

AND THE

RIGHTS OF THE UNLEARNED

———••———

PART FIRST

THE PLEA STATED, ARGUED, AND ILLUSTRATED

THERE are departments of knowledge in reference to which the great bulk of even well-educated men must be content to accept conclusions on the authority of others. Astronomy may be named as an example. The observations and calculations of astronomers belong to a region which is as a *terra incognita* to the mass of mankind. But the soundness of the Copernican theory of the solar system, which underlies them, and of the laws of gravitation which are associated with the names of Newton, Halley, and Kepler, and which are the bases of astronomical calculations, is proved to the perfect conviction of all men by results, the truth and accuracy of which need no demonstration but that of the naked eye. The most

popular and least scientific calendars which we can
purchase for a few pence at the beginning of any year,
tell us, for example, what eclipses of the sun and
moon will take place during the year, the extent of
the eclipse, the moment of its commencement, the
moment of its ending; and the parts of our earth's
surface where the eclipse will be seen. The astronomical prediction never fails of accomplishment;
and the authors of it may be called Experts, as
distinguished from those who cannot follow their
processes and must content themselves with results.

It scarcely needs remark, and yet the remark must
be made, and we shall soon find it of importance, that
there is no true analogy between such experts and
those who call themselves, or rather who are called,
experts in biblical or literary criticism. There are
two departments, it is true, which those who are not
versed in the original languages of Holy Scripture
must relegate to those who are. These are textual
criticism and translation. The very first concern of
the late revisers of our English Bible was to settle
the *Texts*[1] which they were to translate; and in their
prefaces they have explained the principles on which
they proceeded. The Old Testament revisers tell us
that their difficulties in this matter were greater than
those of the New Testament revisers, and they thought

---

[1] The general rule adopted by both the Old Testament
revisers and the New is expressed in the same words, 'That
the Text to be adopted be that for which the evidence is
decidedly preponderating.'

it 'most prudent (they say) to adopt the Massoretic (the Received) Text, as the basis of their work.' So far as known MSS. of the Old Testament are concerned, it seems to be admitted that there is little prospect of much further light being thrown on the subject. Hopes are entertained, however, though not with much confidence, that a more thorough study of the ancient versions – the Greek, Syriac, Coptic, Armenian, and Latin—may result in some improvement of the Text. As to the New Testament, the means of attaining certainty are much greater than in the case of the Old. And 'a revision of the Greek Text was the necessary foundation of the work ' of the revisers ; but they say 'it did not fall within their province to construct a continuous and complete Greek Text.' The main principles by which they were guided are fully explained in their preface.

This is a matter which the unlearned, the non-Hebraists and non-Grecians, must leave in other hands than their own. But in doing so they do not suffer any material disadvantage in their endeavour to understand Holy Scripture. Consider these points :

1. The number of Hebrew scholars who are capable and have the opportunity of original textual investigation is after all comparatively small.

2. The subject of their special study does not admit of the possibility of a unanimous consensus, as in a matter of science, even on the part of the most select and most skilful of textual critics.

3. The results of textual criticism, whatever they may be, and with whatever doubt or confidence they may be asserted, are not hidden from the uninitiated, but soon become the possession of the world at large. To these considerations another has to be added, the force of which will be recognized at once, namely ;

4. That the accumulated experiences of the past in this department confirm our confidence in the substantial trustworthiness of the texts which are represented in our English translation, and leave no room for the expectation that the future will produce any material change. Christians are sometimes alarmed by being told of an enormous number of ' various readings' in Greek manuscripts of the New Testament. But it is a false alarm, as any one may discover for himself if he will only observe the few, and, with scarcely an exception, trifling, changes which the revisers have found necessary.

A learned commentator on Homer, discussing the ' various readings ' in the great Greek epic, the *Iliad*, illustrates his subject by an incidental reference to the various readings of the Greek New Testament. ' For the most part (he says) a mere variety in the position of the words, or in the method of spelling, in the presence or omission of the article, or a change in some insignificant epithet, is all the fruit that weeks and months consumed in the laborious work of comparing old manuscripts can boast of; and when we find a learned man like Wetstein devoting his whole life to the comparison of such insignificant

variations of the Greek Text as our New Testament
exhibits, we are inclined almost to withhold our pity
from him, when we find him complaining that, after
long years spent in adjusting the sacred text, he had
got as his reward only " weak eyes and a disqualifi-
cation for every other pursuit." '

It is not to be inferred, however, that the labours
of textual critics are wasted. Far from it. Every
correction, the smallest, which is effected by them,
is worth the pains which have produced it. And,
above all, ' The negative results are of the utmost
consequence. The Christian world knows, with
a confidence which were otherwise impossible, that
the book which contains the charter of its inheritance
has lived through centuries, undamaged in all essen-
tials, whether from the blundering of ignorant copyists,
or the falsification of unscrupulous partisans [1].'

It will thus be seen that the unlearned share the
fruits of learning, and are not practically damaged
by their dependence on others in the department of
textual criticism.

The same line of argument may be followed with
reference to their dependence on others for the
translation of Holy Scripture, and it need not be
repeated. Those who can read the Hebrew and
Greek originals for themselves have a certain advantage over others, in that the original often produces a more vivid and more suggestive impression
than the familiar English produces. But unless

[1] *Homer and the Iliad.* By John Stuart Blackie. Vol. i. 336.

Hebrew and Greek had become universal languages, the greater part of mankind must of necessity depend on translations. And it is an instructive fact that the Jews, the Hebrews themselves, in the time of Christ, especially those of the Dispersion, were more familiar with a translation, than with the originals which had come down to them in the tongue of their fathers. These originals were very sacred, and held a place to which no translation could aspire. But the Greek Septuagint was in general use, and though it was not inspired, and was far from being a correct translation, apostles did not hesitate to quote it, as we quote our English, as the word of God.

This is a fact of no mean importance. It does not diminish the reverence that is due to the words that were written by prophets and apostles, and which must ever be regarded as the final court of appeal, but it justifies the right of translation, and proves the possibility of conveying, truly and sufficiently, the Divine meaning of the originals to those to whom the originals are a sealed book. The memorable doctrine which Christ announced to the woman of Samaria has a bearing on languages as well as on places. They that worship the Father in spirit and in truth are not dependent on the tongues of Jerusalem and Gerizim for their knowledge of Him or for their power of worship. The apostles on the day of Pentecost knew that the good news which they were inspired to proclaim was as true and Divine in all the languages that were native to the devout men from every nation under heaven, as it was to the home-born men of Jerusalem who had heard the voice of Christ Himself. On the basis of this fact Bible Societies rest. The day of Pentecost is their model, and by means of the printing-press they essay to do for all nations and for all ages, what the apostles did on that day for the multitude around them. Their work will be completed only when the joyous echo comes from the whole wide world, 'We do read, every man in his own tongue, the wonderful works of God.'

We now turn to the Book itself, to ascertain whether it indicates any incapacity on the part of those who receive it to understand it, or any indication of an authority standing between them and the Book, to prescribe the sense in which its words are to be understood. Here the way is clear before us. Moses spoke with authority, but he interposed no authority between himself and the people. There needed none. 'This commandment which I command thee this day, it is not hidden from thee [R.V. it is not too hard for thee], neither is it far off. It is not in heaven, that thou shouldest say, Who shall go up for us to heaven, and bring it unto us, that we may hear it, and do it? Neither is it beyond the sea, that thou shouldest say, Who shall go over the sea for us, and bring it unto us, that we may hear it, and do it? But the word is very nigh unto thee, in thy mouth, and in thy heart, that thou mayest do it ' (Deut. xxx. 11-14). These words were not addressed to a select class, but to the assembled nation. The statutes and judgements with reference to which Moses said, ' I call heaven and earth to record this day, that I have set before you life and death ' (ver. 19), were to be ' taught diligently ' even to children (Deut. vi. 4-9). At the end of every seven years, ' in the solemn year of release,' it was ordained that the law should be publicly read before ' all Israel.' ' Gather the people together (the Law-giver said), men, and women, and children, and thy stranger that is within thy gates, that they may hear, and that they may learn, and fear the Lord your God, and observe to do all the words of this law ! ' (Deut. xxxi. 10-12). The priests and the elders of the people were charged with the fulfilment of this ordinance, but were invested with no authority besides. When Ezra read ' the book of the law of Moses, which the Lord had commanded to Israel,' to the ' men and women ' who had returned from exile, we are told that ' they gave the sense, and caused the people to understand the reading' (Neh. viii. 1, 8). This probably means that they translated the Hebrew of Moses into the Aramaic dialect which the people now spoke. It may mean likewise that Ezra and the priests who aided him in this memorable work, expounded to the people as they read the requirements of the law with its promises and threatenings. But exposition implied no authority then any more than it does now.

What is true of the teaching of Moses is true of the teaching of prophets. They too spoke with Divine authority; but between their words and the people there stood no one to tell the people how they must understand them. 'Write the vision (the Lord said to Habakkuk), and make it plain upon tables, that he may run that readeth it' (ii. 2). When the vision became at any time as 'the words of a book that was sealed,' it was not that they were hard to understand, but because the people would have it so (Isa. xxix. 9–16).

Reference may be made in this connexion, though it is scarcely necessary, to the Jewish fable of an oral law by which the written law was to be interpreted. The Talmud says that during the whole day while Moses continued on the mount, he was learning the written law, but at night he was occupied in receiving another law explanatory of the first, which he was commanded not to commit to writing, but to hand down by oral tradition. When Jerusalem was taken by the Romans, and the temple destroyed, and the nation scattered abroad, it was feared, we are told, that the traditionary law might be lost, and therefore it was resolved to preserve it by committing it to writing. This was done by 'Judah the holy,' about the middle of the second century of our era. Hence the Talmud.

Over against this story we need only recite the words of the history of the law-giving : 'Moses came

and told the people *all* the words of the Lord ; . . . and
Moses *wrote* all the words of the Lord ' (Exod. xxiv.
3, 4). Throughout the entire history of the nation
from that time onward to the latest of the prophets,
we search in vain for a single phrase or allusion that
might indicate the existence of any other than the
written law. And when in the Gospels we find
references to traditions of the fathers, we still find
no appeal to an oral law contemporaneous with the
written. The traditions were only the comments of
Rabbinical teachers, and their general effect was to
make void the one Law which alone bore the seal
of God.

If we turn to the New Testament we still look
in vain for the existence of an authority, outside
its own pages, to determine for the reader how
he should understand the apostolic words. The
matter may be tested by a reference to the Epistles
of St. Paul. This great apostle possessed and claimed
the authority of Christ for his teaching. He knew
' the mind of Christ.' A dispensation of the gospel
was committed to him (1 Cor. ix. 17). By revelation
there was made known to him the mystery of Christ
(Eph. iii. 2–7). What he preached and what he
wrote bore the seal of the Lord whose ambassador
he was. But between Paul and his hearer or reader
there stood no authoritative interpreter. To the
Corinthian Church, the fellow Christians of ' all that
called upon the name of Jesus Christ our Lord in

every place' (1 Cor. i. 2), he said, 'Judge ye (ye who read my words) what I say' (x. 15).

The Epistle to the Romans is often described as the most *theological* of all the apostle's writings, and it may be assumed that it was to 'some things' in this Epistle that his fellow apostle Peter referred, when he spoke of 'some things hard to be understood, which the ignorant and unsteadfast wrest, as they do also the other scriptures, unto their own destruction' (2 Pet. iii. 16, R.V.). But neither apostle prescribed, nor suggested the existence of, any intermediary to save even the ignorant and unsteadfast from wresting the Scriptures; an intermediary who should impair the right or diminish the responsibility of those whom they addressed. The readers of the apostolic epistles were, many of them, Jews who carried into the Christian Church prejudices which were to them as a second nature; and many of them heathens who found it equally hard to rid themselves of old superstitions and habits. But the apostles treated them all as capable of understanding their reasons against a Judaic ritualism, as in the Epistle to the Galatians; and against heathen corruptions and heathen philosophies as in the Epistles to the Corinthians and to the Colossians; and they held their readers personally responsible for the right understanding of their instructions.

Christian readers of to-day are not less capable than were those of the first century to understand the apostolic writings; nor are they less responsible

personally for the understanding and practice of the
will of Christ, as authoritatively declared by His
immediately commissioned ambassadors.

The rejection of the claim of any body calling itself
' The Church,' or of councils presuming to speak in
the name of the Church, to come between us and the
written inspired word with an authoritative declaration
of the meaning of the word, is not to be construed
as a rejection of the *aids* which we may derive from
the studies of those who have gone before us—the
fathers of bygone ages—or our own contemporaries.
Such a rejection would be the sign not of a true independence, but of self-willed conceit and arrogance.

If we are right so far, we see (1) that ordinary
readers of Holy Scripture enjoy all the benefits of
the light which a learning not their own can throw
on the original texts of both the Old and the New
Testament; and (2) that through translation they
enjoy practically all the advantage which those possess
who can read the Scriptures in Hebrew or in Greek.
We have seen likewise (3) that the books themselves
recognize no authority as standing between them and
their readers. The attempt to assert such authority
issued, in the case of the Old Testament, not in
enforcing, but in making void the Divine law. And
the case of the New is not very different. If the
apostles had risen from the dead four or six centuries
after their lifetime—the age to which some would
have us bow as authoritative,—their language of

sorrow and amazement would have been, 'We marvel
that ye are so far removed from us unto another
gospel and other ordinances.'

But may there not have been developed in our
times another class of experts, to whose learning and
wisdom it will be expedient that we bow? If so, we
have to ask who they are and how we shall know
them? Are they the men who have attained to
a very high knowledge of the language in which
prophets spoke and wrote, and of all that can con-
tribute, directly or indirectly, to the understanding
of the writings of the Old Testament? Do these
constitute a class who are entitled to impose their
interpretations on the world? Here we are met
at once with an initial difficulty. These very learned
men are divided into two irreconcileable and antagon-
istic forces, on the very questions in regard to which
the unlearned are supposed at present to need
guidance. The one party find in their learning
a confirmation of what is called, though not with
strict accuracy, the traditional theory of the Old
Testament; the theory which was held — not as
a theory, but as an unquestioned fact, through the
age of Christ and His apostles until a very recent
period—that the five books commonly ascribed to
Moses were rightly ascribed to him, and that in
these books we have the very foundation of the
Jewish polity and of the Jewish history. The
other party find in their learning reason to deny

this theory, root and branch, and to maintain that the true beginnings of Judaism and its theology are to be found in the prophets of the eighth century before Christ, and that the histories and laws, with some fragmentary exceptions, which precede these in the book, are due to authors of the prophetic age, and did not attain their present completed form, especially in the matter of law-giving, till after the Babylonian exile.   These two classes of the 'learned' are fundamentally contrary the one to the other, and we cannot bow the knee to both.

The idea of authoritative experts based on Hebrew learning is exploded by the fact of this fundamental difference.   Neither class has a right to an authority which is not conceded to the other.   And perhaps it may be said with truth that neither claims or asserts any such right.   But it is claimed or asserted for one of them.   It has become a fashion on the part of many to regard the scholars who have adopted the new theories regarding the Old Testament as experts, to the exclusion of scholars who are equally learned ; and it is to them alone we are told to look for a verdict on those problems which are to be taken out of the hands of the people.   But why should these be invested with a critical dictatorship?

(1) They do not themselves claim a personal superiority in scholarship over many who differ from them. They may mourn over their learned brethren who ' will not come to the light ' which has shone on their minds, but they do not deny their equal capacity.

(2) Some of the most eminent of them confess that the ultimate decision of great Old Testament problems does not depend after all on scholarship. One of them (Dr. Cheyne) has said emphatically, with reference to a question which he has made very specially his own—that of the second portion of Isaiah—that the decision of the critical question will mainly depend on other than purely linguistic considerations. As to the fifty-third of Isaiah, he says that the question of its true meaning rests less with the critic than with the heart and judgement of the Christian. Dean Farrar, who accepts one of the most painfully destructive, and, as I think, one of the least tenable, conclusions of the Higher Criticism, in the matter of the Book of Daniel, remarks on the uncertainty of the results that are attained on purely philological grounds, and refers to the fact that two Hebraists, so profound as Ewald and Hitzig, take such opposite views of language that the one can feel sure that the second Psalm is of Davidic, and the other of Maccabean origin (*On the Minor Prophets*, p. 104). Kuenen confesses that he has no data for his critical speculations that are not equally possessed by all who have the Bible in their hands. Prof. Robertson Smith is equally explicit. 'We have (he says) almost no contemporary helps for the study of Hebrew antiquity beyond the books which were received into the Hebrew Canon' (*The Old Testament in the Jewish Church*, p. 17).

(3) There is a third reason why we should dis-

allow anything like a dictatorship to those who are ordinarily called Higher Critics, and that is the extraordinary differences in the results at which they arrive, while starting from and building on the same critical principles.

As to the old and ever-new question of the right of private judgement in its many bearings—the right of every man to think for himself and to act for himself in his relations to his Maker—enough to say that the denial of the right by man or magistrate, Church or Churchman, throws on the denier the duty of proving his right to deny.   And how is that to be proved ? Only by proving the possession of authority from Heaven.   And the attempt to prove this is itself an appeal to the private judgement of those whom it is designed to convince.   It cannot be forgotten that even prophets were not entitled to be heard unless they were in a position to prove their prophetic authority.   And Christ Himself did not demand hearing or faith without giving abundant evidence that He had a right to speak in the name of God.   If He had not done in Israel works such as no man had ever done before, He said, the nation would have been without sin in rejecting His claims.   Even a Divine Revelation, then, appeals to the private, the personal, judgement, including the conscience and entire spiritual nature of those whom it addresses ; acknowledges their right, apart from authoritative interference by any one, to consider its claims, and throws on them the responsibility of a decision. It may be called an awful right; and it is certainly an awful responsibility. An inspired apostle sums up the logical conclusion when he says, ' To his own (the only) Master (Lord of the conscience) he standeth or falleth.'

Before proceeding further it may be well to explain that I use the term ' Higher Critics ' only in the sense in which it is now popularly bandied about—not meaning thereby critics who have brought criticism to bear on subjects which have been hitherto free from its scope, such as the origin of the books, the original text of the books, the meaning of the books —with everything external to the books and internal, that can throw any light upon them [1]: but critics who by certain processes, whether legitimate or illegitimate, have come to the conclusion that all the ages until very recently have been entirely mistaken with reference to the authorship, and historical or non-historical character, of the five books which are the foundation of our Bible, and of certain other books as well. This criticism is in no proper sense higher or superior, nor are its advocates superior, nor its results. It does not

---

[1] ' Properly speaking the Higher Criticism is an inquiry into the object and character of the writings to which it is applied. It seeks to ascertain by all available means the authors by whom, the time at which, the circumstances under which, and the design with which they were produced. Such investigations rightly conducted must prove a most important aid to the understanding and just appreciation of the writings in question.'—Dr. W. H. Green.

raise us to a plane of thought or knowledge that is in
any sense higher.   And when it claims to be historical
we are reminded of a passage in one of Mr. John
Bright's great speeches : ' He remarked, we are told,
that Mr.——— seemed to read a different history from
anybody else, or that he made his own history, and,
like Voltaire, made it better without facts than with
them.'

The reader may better understand what follows if
reminded that the critics, whose position I contest,
divide the legislation of the books which we call
Mosaic mainly into three codes.   The first is the
Covenant Code, which is brief, and may be allowed
to be really Mosaic, namely, Exod. xx–xxiii.   The
second is the Deuteronomic Code, consisting of the
laws which are found in Deuteronomy, which belong,
not to the age of Moses, but to an age probably some
eight centuries later.   The third is the Levitical or
Priestly Code, which we find in the later chapters of
Exodus, in the whole of Leviticus, and spread over
some ten chapters of the Book of Numbers.   This code,
none of which, it is held, comes from Moses, was of
gradual growth, and did not attain its present propor-
tions till the time of Ezra.

PART SECOND

THE PLEA CONFIRMED BY THE CONSIDERATION
OF REASONS WHICH ARE INDEPENDENT OF
EXPERT SCHOLARSHIP

BEING then free, and bound to judge for themselves
with such aids as are within the reach of ordinary
thoughtful readers of Holy Scripture, non-experts are
not without abundant material whereon to form an
intelligent judgement respecting questions which some
would take out of their hands and reserve for a favoured
class, whom they would invest with a quasi-critical
dictatorship.

FIRST OF ALL : **They cannot help being struck
with the fact that the new theory would displace
convictions which have come down unchallenged
from the earliest Jewish age until what may
be called yesterday.** These convictions have been
ever regarded as facts, and as having been confirmed
in the course of the ages by prophets and apostles and
by the Lord of both.

According to the so-called Higher Criticism, it is
maintained that ' the Books of Moses have been falsely

ascribed to him, and were in reality produced at a much
later period.   It is affirmed that the history is by no
means reliable, and merely records the uncertain and
variant traditions of a past Mosaic age ; and that the
laws are not those of Moses, but the growth of centuries
after his time.'   We meet this averment by an appeal
to the principle laid down by the commentator on
Homer whom we have already quoted.   After discussing the detailed and specific reasons which F. A.
Wolf and others assigned for denying the unity of the
Iliad, and the popular conception of its authorship,
he says, ' We who stand on the received text have the
tradition of long centuries in our favour, and not one
substantial reason against us.   Possession, in literary
as in civil matters, is nine points of the law ; and
he who wishes to shake an old received document
out of its consistency, must be prepared to bring
something more weighty to bear against it than clever
guesses and well-devised possibilities [1].'

In substance this argument of the learned professor
holds good with reference to the Mosaic authorship
of the Pentateuch and its legislation.   We are as
men '*in possession*, who have the tradition of long
centuries in our favour.'   ' It is an admitted rule of
all sound criticism,' says Canon Rawlinson, ' that
books are to be regarded as proceeding from the
writers whose names they bear, unless very strong
reasons indeed can be adduced to the contrary'
(*Bampton Lectures*, p. 39).   This rule applies to the

[1] *Homer and the Iliad.* By John Stuart Blackie. Vol. i. 239.

authorship of the *Iliad* and *Odyssey*, the *Aeneid*, the *Commentaries de Bello Gallico*, Xenophon's *Expedition of Cyrus*, and a multitude besides. 'These books do not bear their authors' names in the direct form in which a modern title-page declares an author's name. But the age to which they belonged believed in a certain authorship, and later ages have accepted and transmitted the belief.'

The critic may say that we beg the question when we assert that the tradition of Mosaic authorship can be traced to the age of the events which the books profess to record. But he cannot deny that the books themselves purport, sometimes explicitly, at all times implicitly, to be at least a contemporary record of the events which they record. Even Kuenen writes : 'It is not only the superscriptions that assign the laws to Moses and locate them in the desert, but the form of the legislation likewise accords with this determina-tion and place. Now this may be explained in two ways : either the laws really come from Moses and the desert, or they are merely put into his mouth, and the desert and so forth belong to their literary form and presentment.' The latter alternative the critics choose. Moses was not the author. The laws were put into his mouth in after centuries. And the incidents, circumstances, and colouring of the desert are mere fiction, fabricated as a false setting for the purpose of giving effect to these laws, and thus investing them with an authority to which they had no right.

The bearing of these bold assertions of dishonesty on the part of the authors of the Pentateuch will be considered farther on.   Meantime we have to do only with the acknowledgement that the testimony of the books themselves, whether true or false, is unmistakable.

Onward from the days of Moses to the days of Malachi, there are direct references to the statutes which lay at the foundation of the national polity, and other references, threatenings and promises, which pre-suppose the Mosaic legislation of the Pentateuch, and which are utterly unintelligible on the hypothesis that that legislation was not yet in existence.   All this has been set forth elaborately by many writers. And the argument is valid that the silence of history during considerable periods of the nation's existence is no proof that Mosaic statutes were not observed; and if it could be proved that they were not observed, this non-observance would be no proof that they had not been given.   In fact, the perpetual complaint of prophets was that their people had forsaken the law of their God, and had followed the devices of their own evil hearts.

Without attempting to trace the story of the book in detail, the reader's attention may be called to two or three marked epochs in the Jewish annals. David charged Solomon, not merely to keep certain laws which he ascribed to Moses, but to keep all that was 'written' in a certain book which was known as 'The Law of Moses' (1 Kings ii. 1-3).   David must

have had this book in his hand when he celebrated
the glory of God which the heavens declared to him
as he shepherded his father's flock on the plains of
Bethlehem, and when he celebrated with no less
enthusiasm the statutes of the Lord which rejoiced
his heart, which were more to be desired than gold,
and in keeping of which there was great reward. Where
did David find this law of the Lord? It must have
come to him through the great judge and prophet of
his age. And if we ask where Samuel found it, we
must go back to find a possible beginning, from
generation to generation till we reach the days of
Moses.

Three hundred years after the days of Solomon we
come to the reign of Hezekiah, of whom it is said that
he kept the 'commandments which the Lord commanded Moses' (2 Kings xviii. 6). And within a few
verses we are told that the King of Assyria carried
away Israel unto Assyria 'because they obeyed not the
voice of the Lord their God, but transgressed His
covenant, and all that Moses the servant of the Lord
commanded, and would not hear them, nor do them.'
It is plain that the commandments of the Lord by
Moses must have been in a book, and that this book
was at this time in the hands of both Judah and Israel.

The greatest of the prophets ministered in the days
of Hezekiah. And it is not a matter of mere inference
that he must have regarded the commandments which
Hezekiah kept so faithfully as the commandments of
Moses, and the book which recorded them as the

book of Moses.   A mistake on the part of Hezekiah would have been the mistake of Isaiah as well.   In the book written by himself, Moses is named only in one passage (Isa. lxiii. 11–14), and that incidentally, and yet in a way which implies all that the preceding history ascribes to him as the leader of the people out of Egypt and in the wilderness.   So that here we have another illustration of the *implicit* testimony of the prophets to the law of Moses.

The story of the finding of the book of the law in the house of the Lord, when the temple was being repaired, belongs to the reign of Hezekiah's great-grandson, Josiah, and is recorded in 2 Kings xxii and 2 Chron. xxxiv.   The version of this story imagined by the Higher Criticism will be considered in a later chapter.   At present we are only noting some principal epochs at which we find express mention of the law of Moses.   There is nothing improbable in the account of the matter.   The reign of Josiah's grandfather, Manasseh, had extended over more than half a century, and was distinguished by a virulent spread of idolatry, by the most cruel persecution of the faithful, and the most outrageous profanation of the sanctuary.   Manasseh's son, Amon, served the idols which his father had for a brief season forsaken.   And to this long inheritance of corruption Josiah succeeded when he was only eight years of age.   Hezekiah's copy of the law, written according to the requirements of Moses, made seventy-five years before the reign of Josiah, was most probably destroyed during the fierce persecutions of the reign of Manasseh. And there is nothing strange in the supposition that Josiah had not seen a complete copy of the Pentateuch till it was found by Hilkiah, the high priest.

When we come to the days of Ezra and Malachi we find express mention of the law of Moses on the return of the exiles under Ezra, and still later in the last prophetic writings of the Old Testament. Even if there were more lapses of silence than there are in the history, the words of Malachi are conclusive evidence of the existence of the Mosaic origin of the Pentateuch, of at least a portion of it which is now the matter of dispute. ' Remember ye the law of Moses My servant, which I commanded unto him in Horeb for all Israel, with the statutes and judgements.'

The identity of the book which we call the law of Moses, and which we find mentioned in the several instances which have been quoted, and in many others, may be illustrated by a familiar example. Bede wrote his *Ecclesiastical History of the English Nation* about the year 730 A. D. Suppose we found a reference to Bede's *Ecclesiastical History of the English Nation* in 1230 A. D., and another in 1430 A.D., and another in 1630 A.D.; we should conclude that the book referred to was one and the same, unless some strong and strange evidence was forthcoming that the original book had been destroyed or lost, and that a spurious production, a forgery, in fact, had taken its place. Why not accept on the same principle the fact of the identity of the Law of Moses from the beginning? The words

of Malachi may justly be regarded as a final confirmation of earlier prophetic words, a summing up of
the witness of many ages.

The four centuries which separated Malachi from
Christ were far from being what they seem to many
readers of the Bible—a great historic blank. They
were most eventful in the external relations of the Jews
to the Persian Empire, the Macedonian Alexander
and the growing Roman power. And they include
specially an event which made the sacred books of
the Jews accessible to the civilized world outside their
own nation, the translation of these books into the
language which the conquests of Alexander had made
wellnigh universal, or at least universally understood
so far as book-learning was concerned. The exact
date or dates of the translation, the persons of the
translators, and the immediate occasions or motives
of the work may be matters of some controversy. But
the Septuagint is a fact of great moment, and it comes
to us from the age of which we have no Biblical history.
Whatever may be its imperfections or errors, it bears
witness to the continued existence of the book two
hundred or two hundred and fifty years after Malachi,
and it was sufficiently true to the original Hebrew to gain
general acceptance among the Jews themselves. So
that in the time of Christ we have the Old Testament
in its primitive form held most sacred, and with im-
punity not to be tampered with, and in a translated
form which became to a large extent the popular
Bible. Christ had both in His hands, the original

certainly, which alone was read in the synagogue
worship. The deductions which we draw from the
fact that He did not challenge its integrity or its
authority will be considered in another chapter. We
are now only tracing the existence of the book, the
book which begins with Genesis and the early Mosaic
history of the people of Israel and ends with the
prophecy of Malachi. We need not trace it farther.
From henceforth it was under the guardianship of
both Jews and Christians, or rather of Him who was
the Divine Angel of the Old Covenant and is the
Divine Lord of the New.

It will now be seen with what entire confidence we
may adopt the argument of the Greek scholar, who,
while willing to appraise and discuss every objection
which the ingenuity of Wolf and others could allege
against the Homeric authorship of the *Iliad*, argued
that 'the tradition of long centuries' was not to be
set aside by 'clever guesses and well-devised possibilities.' On this ground alone the case in support
of the Mosaic origin of the law and of the books
which contain it, is immensely stronger than that in
support of the reputed traditional origin of any other
ancient book. Had we only such evidence, partly
explicit and partly implicit, as may be gathered from
the writings of the Son of Sirach [1], Philo, Josephus, and

---

[1] The Son of Sirach, the author of the book known in the
Apocrypha as 'Ecclesiasticus,' who wrote from B.C. 200–150,
was familiar with the classification of the books as the Law, the
Psalms, the Prophets. Philo, in Egypt, in the age of Christ

others, it would be of a kind with that which guarantees to us the authenticity of other ancient books, and it would be difficult to resist its historic validity. We have all this in the case of the Bible books whose origin we are considering. But we have a great deal more, a distinctly divine tradition, which lifts them to an altogether higher plane.

Himself, wrote large commentaries on the Old Testament. The very specific testimony of Josephus, who wrote after the destruction of Jerusalem, may be given in full : 'We have not a countless number of books, discordant and arrayed against each other, but only *two-and-twenty books*, containing the history of every age, which are justly accredited as divine [old editions of Josephus read merely, 'which are justly accredited'—θεῖα comes from Eusebius' transcript of Josephus in *Eccl. Hist.* iii. 10]; and of these, *five* belong to Moses, which contain both the laws and the history of the generations of men until his death. This period lacks but little of 3,000 years. From the death of Moses, moreover, until the reign of Artaxerxes [Eusebius—'from the death of Moses to that of Artaxerxes'; and so most of the Codices, omitting ἀρχῆς, reign], king of the Persians after Xerxes, the prophets who followed Moses have described the things which were done during the age of each one respectively, in *thirteen* books. The remaining *four* contain hymns to God and rules of life for men. From the time of Artaxerxes, moreover, until our present period all occurrences have been written down ; *but they are not regarded as entitled to the like credit with those which precede them, because there was no certain succession of prophets.* Fact has shown what confidence we place in our own writings. For although so many ages have passed away, no one has dared to add to them, nor to take anything from, nor to make alterations. In all Jews it is implanted, even from their birth, to regard them as being the instructions of God, and to abide steadfastly by them, and, if it be necessary, to die gladly for them.'

SECONDLY : **The unlearned reader of Holy Scripture may well stand in doubt of a theory which, to say the least, places the testimony of Christ in a very ambiguous position.**

Why I bring the testimony of our Lord into the foreground, instead of reserving it to confirm other arguments, will appear as we proceed. The materials for a judgement regarding it are spread over the four gospels, and, were it not that difficulties have been raised or suggested, one might say boldly, 'The man may read that holds the plough.' Without controversy, it may be said, that the learned and unlearned stand on the same level in regard to it. There are no various readings and no various translations to require a verdict on the part of experts. Even with reference to the apostolic words in Phil. ii. 6–8, which have been brought into prominence in relation to the subject, scholars are agreed as to the fittest translation, and we have it in the Revised Version. The bearing of the apostle's words on the condition of Christ in His humiliation is to be determined, not on speculative grounds, but in the light of the facts of His life, which lie before us in the gospels 'without a veil.' The reverent reader and learner turns to these facts, to ascertain whether Christ pronounced any judgement on those Scriptures whose origin and authorship are at present in dispute, and what that judgement was.

1. It is not denied that the Old Testament, as we have it, was in all substantial respects the scripture or scriptures which Christ and the generation to which He belonged held in their hands, and which were read in their public Sabbatic worship. Even if we accepted the Higher Critical theory, it would still be true that our Old Testament in its entireness was anterior to the days of Christ, and that it was Christ's own Bible.

2. It is not denied that Christ was intimately familiar with the contents of His Bible. In conversation with His disciples and in discussions with the Jews, He had occasion to refer to facts and sayings that are scattered over the Old Testament from the first verses in Genesis to the last in Malachi[1].

3. In our Lord's references to the Old Testament it is important to observe (1) that in no instance did He quote from books not found in our Bible or from oral tradition ; and (2) that there are books in our Bible from which He did not quote, or at least of which there is no record that He quoted. This is easily accounted for. His recorded quotations from the Old Testament were incidental, i. e. as occasion arose through circumstances, and through questions and objections on the part of the people or on the part of disciples.

---

[1] The author has illustrated this in detail in articles in the *Evangelical Magazine* for May, June, and July, 1896 ; and he avails himself occasionally of what will be found more fully in these articles.

4. In addition to specific facts and books, Christ, especially after His resurrection, placed the seal of His authority on the entire collection, under designations by which it was popularly known, such as the law, the prophets, and the Psalms (Luke xxiv. 44). 'Beginning at Moses and all the prophets, He expounded unto them in all the scriptures the things concerning Himself' (Luke xxiv. 27). Would, we naturally exclaim, that the evangelist had recorded the gracious and precious words in which Christ traced Himself from the beginning to the end of the ancient scriptures ! But with the key to these scriptures which He supplied—Himself the mystery which has been veiled for ages—and with the fact that He opened the understandings of His disciples to understand what He told them, we may be sure that the gospel records are in no sense misleading as to His Person and His Mission, and equally sure that the teachings of His apostles, to whom He promised the guidance of the Holy Spirit, were in entire accordance with His own words. Searching the Scriptures for ourselves, it is a matter of the deepest interest that we can find Him unveiled in the very earliest of them, as the seed of the woman who should bruise the serpent's head, and in the very latest of them as 'The LORD,' 'The Lord of hosts,' who should suddenly come to His temple—these two prophecies binding, not by accident, but by Divine purpose, into a grand consistent whole, those revelations which had been given, at sundry times and in

divers manners, through at least four millenniums
of fallen man's existence on the earth.

5. There is another fact which lies prominently
on the face of the gospel records, this, namely, that
Christ spoke with conscious authority.   This authority
may be described as both delegated and personal.
Of His delegated authority He spoke with frequent
emphasis.   'The word which ye hear is not Mine,
but the Father's which sent Me.'   He stood before
His countrymen in Galilee and Judea, visibly only
as Jesus of Nazareth.   Hence it was that when the
Jews marvelled and said, ' How knoweth this man
letters, having never learned ?' Jesus said, ' My doctrine is not Mine, but His that sent Me.'   And yet the
very terms in which He thus disclaimed a personal,
i. e. in this case a human, a merely human, origin and
authorship for His doctrine, pointed to something in
His underlying personal relation to His doctrine very
different from the relation in which prophets stood to
theirs. The difference between Christ and the prophets
was not one of degree merely, the difference between
a partial and what has been called a ' complete
endowment of manhood,' such as is indicated in
the statement that God gave not the Spirit by
measure to Him.   His was a personal authority, such
as neither prophet nor apostle dared to assume.
Standing before the multitude with the clear memory
of all the Divine teaching which the nation had
enjoyed for ages, and of Divine pronouncements
against such as claimed authority unauthorized, and

with a full knowledge of great contemporary inter-
preters of the law, and of men of the immediately
preceding age, of whom the nation was proud and
in whom the nation trusted—standing there in
spiritual majesty and conscious of all that His
words involved in relation both to God and to man,
He repeats, through every point of His exposition of
what had been said to them of old, this, and this
only, ' I say unto you.' If man never spake like
this man, it is because never before was there man
like this man. How else could He say, ' Heaven and
earth shall pass away ; but My words shall not pass
away ' (Luke xxi. 33) ?

6. We may assume as a fact, although some would
call it an inference or deduction, that Christ regarded
the Old Testament incidents which He quoted, and
on which He based arguments or lessons, not as myths
or fables or allegories or uncertain national traditions,
but as historically true and real. Beginning with the
creation of man and woman and the primitive law of
marriage, we read the story of His references onward
till we come to His recognition of the foretelling of
the coming of a prophet in the spirit of Elijah ; and
we find no room in His words for legendary or
allegorical hypotheses. Abel, Noah, Abraham, Moses,
Elijah, Jonah, and Daniel, were regarded by Him
as real personages ; and if the incidents which He
quotes, such as the death of Abel, the Flood, the
burning bush, the brazen serpent, the ministry of
Elijah in the reign of Ahab, the mission of Jonah

to Nineveh, and the prophecy of Daniel respecting
Himself, were not realities, and are not truthfully
narrated, He was mistaken.

7. If this be granted, it can scarcely be denied
that Christ regarded the books from which He quoted
as truthful and trustworthy. The facts and sayings
which He quoted cannot be isolated from the con-
nexions in which they stand. They are not aphorisms
whose truth is in themselves, and which would be true
even if spoken by the Devil, as nuggets of gold are
gold even if found in a mass of rubbish. The ground
on which Christ requires His hearers to accept them,
apart from His comments and interpretations, is that
they found them in the written law of the Lord.
'Have ye not read?' or 'It is written,' is the ground of
His constant appeal. The acknowledged authority
of the 'written' and 'read' book constituted with
His hearers sufficient and undisputed authority for
the words which He quoted from it.

This being so, I do not see how it can be logically
questioned that every one of the five books of Moses
bears the seal of Christ :—that of Genesis, when, with
reference to the law of marriage, He said, 'Have ye
not read?' (Matt. xix. 4); that of Exodus, when He
said 'Have ye not read?' with reference to the words
of God to Moses out of the burning bush (Matt. xxii. 31
and Luke xx. 37): that of Leviticus, when He instructed
the leper to obey a law of Moses found only in
Leviticus; that of Numbers, when He referred to the

brazen serpent which Moses lifted up by Divine
command; an incident to be found only in Numbers
(John iii. 14); that of Deuteronomy, which Christ
quoted three times with the formula, 'It is written,'
in His conflict with the Tempter (Matt. iv. 4, 7, 10).
The seal put thus on the Book of Deuteronomy is of
more than argumentative interest. In the awful
solitude of His conflict with the Tempter, in the
hour which in some respects was the most critical
in the history of redemption, the Son of God, whose
consciousness of Himself could not be shaken by the
Tempter's insinuation of the doubt, does not at once
put forth the power which could have smitten His
adversary, not into silence merely, but into helpless-
ness. He falls back on written words which had
been light and strength to the saints of many ages,
thus associating Himself with the redeemed of the
past and of the future, His 'brethren' (Heb. ii. 11,
17, 18), and instructing them how to meet and foil
the adversaries of their souls. Was the book which
it is evident had yielded spiritual nourishment to the
Son of Man, while yet He had not entered on the
public discharge of His Divine ministry, and by
which now at the very commencement of His public
life He quenched the subtle darts of the Wicked
One (Eph. vi. 16), other than what it professed to
be, a very record of an important epoch in the
history of God's ancient people, and of words
addressed to them by Divine authority on the eve
of their entrance on national existence in a land

which would be to them a scene of manifold tempta-
tions ?

But there is still more to be said as to the bearing
of our review of Christ's testimony on the question
of the age and authorship of the legislation and books
which have hitherto borne the name of Moses.

The first thing that strikes us is that Christ did
not challenge the national belief in the origin of the
oldest even of their sacred books, and in the authority
which they derived from their supposed connexion
with the man whom they regarded as the very
founder of their national constitution.   This fact
by itself, explain it as you will, is no mean pre-
sumptive evidence that they were right in their
belief.   If they were wrong, they were dominated
by an error which was fundamental, and which could
not but vitiate their spiritual life and mis-direct their
obedience to the Divine will.   Christ, we know, was
in perpetual conflict with the chief sects of the
nation, Sadducees and Pharisees, and with popular
sentiment as well.   The people often listened gladly
to His gracious words, but their opposition, and even
bitter hostility, were as often excited by sayings
which they considered hard, and which offended
their national pride and worldly hopes.   The most
superficial acquaintance with the pages of the gospels
reveals Him as a severely independent and uncompromising Teacher.   He boldly combated the most
cherished Jewish notions.   How came it to pass

that He spared the great error, if error it was, which
the people of His age had inherited from their
fathers, and thus passed it on from the Jewish age
into and through the Christian age, to be discovered
at last only by the penetrating and uncompromising
intellects of these last days? The only conclusion
we can come to, if the honour of Christ is to be
preserved unsullied, is that He did not challenge the
national judgement because it was a true judgement.
He was Himself the Truth, and only truth found
favour with Him.

Let it not be imagined for a moment that the
correctness or incorrectness of the national belief was
a matter of little or no consequence in relation to
Christ's own work and mission ; in other words, that
the testimony of the books to Him was equally valid,
whether they had genuinely come from Moses or
had been fabricated—possibly for a good end, the end
justifying the means—some of them towards the
end of that dispensation which an apostle regarded
as a schoolmaster [1] to lead on the Jewish people to
Christ. We have good reason for saying that Christ
Himself did not think so. There is a sense in which
His Messiahship, His title to the Messiahship, depended

---

[1] The Revised Version (Gal. iii. 24) says ' tutor' instead of
' schoolmaster.' Bishop Lightfoot explains thus : ' The paeda-
gogue, or tutor, frequently a superior slave, was entrusted with
the moral supervision of the child. Thus his office was quite
distinct from that of the teacher. . . . As well in his inferior rank,
as in his recognized duty of enforcing discipline, this person was
a fit emblem of the Mosaic law.'—*On Gal.* iii. 24.

on the genuineness of these ancient scriptures, that is, on the fact that their prophetic witness to Him had the authority of God Himself through His most honoured (see Num. xii. 7, 8) servant, Moses.

In nothing does what we may call the independence and originality of Christ appear so significantly as in the matter of the Messiahship. Both He and the people believed in a Messiah to come ; both believed that the Messiah was foremirrored in their sacred books, and that whosoever claimed the office must make good his title out of these books. But their reading of the books did not result in the same conclusions as to what manner of person the Messiah was to be, and what manner of benefits He should confer on His nation. The people, groaning under a foreign yoke, and reading their Scriptures under the influence of a worldly spirit which could imagine, and aspire after, no higher blessing than national freedom and supremacy, concentrated their thoughts on predictions which foreshadowed the power, dominion, and glory of the Messiah. Consequently 'they expected (to use the words of the author of *Ecce Homo*) to see once more a warrior king, judging in the gate of Jerusalem, or surrounded by his mighty men, or carrying his victorious arms into the neighbouring countries, or receiving submissive embassies from Rome and Seleucia, and in the meantime holding awful communication with Jehovah, administering His law, and singing His praise. It was as impossible for them to conceive the true Christ, to imagine what He would

do, or how He would do it, as it was impossible for
them to fill His place.'

Both before and after Christ there arose men who
were in sympathy with the national spirit, and were
bold enough to present themselves to their people as
the embodiment and realization of the national hope.
But their work soon came to an end.

Jesus of Nazareth, brought up in, and breathing for
thirty years, the feverish atmosphere of Galilean ex-
pectations, was conscious of a Messiahship of another
order.   It was quite natural for His countrymen, when
they witnessed the mysterious power with which He
could feed thousands, a power which had its parallel
only in that which fed the multitude of Israel in the
wilderness, and which they associated with the name
of Moses, to conclude that He was fit to take the
kingship that would secure the victory and freedom
for which they longed.   But He would not have it.
And yet He was a king, and knew it, and boldly
avowed it even in the presence of the representative
of all-powerful Rome, and that when He seemed
Himself to be the most helpless of men.

But how different His kingship from that of popular
expectation ! We may well wonder that He was able
to separate Himself so absolutely from the spirit of
His age and nation.   And we may wonder likewise
that one brought up in the meanness and poverty
of a carpenter's home, should see in Himself or
imagine that He was the One in whom four millenniums of prophecy culminated, and in whom all the

nations of the earth were to be blessed. The secret
of His knowledge is to be found in Himself, in His consciousness of what He was. But how should the people
know? How should their eyes penetrate through
the cloud which hid His glory, and which seemed to
render the existence of any such glory impossible?
He did not ostentatiously or even prominently
proclaim His Messiahship and His Divinity. From
the first He allowed disciples to render Him homage
as the Messiah and the Son of God (John i. 43–51).
And on an occasion which has become memorable,
though one would imagine it the least likely, He made
an express declaration of the fact (John iv. 25, 26).
But for the most part He left what He was, to be
inferred and proved by His works, His teaching, and
His character. Above all, it was necessary that He
should not shrink from an appeal to the books, which,
though much misunderstood, were the true ground and
the true test of the Messianic hope. And this appeal
He made boldly. 'Ye search the Scriptures,' He
said, 'and they are they which testify of Me' (John
v. 39). Of these Scriptures He made special and
emphatic reference to the writings of Moses; and this
reference is of first importance. It is often slurred
over by saying that Christ might describe a book, as
we often do, simply by the name of its reputed author.
But no escape can be found in this idea from the
unmistakable force of these words : 'Had ye believed
Moses, ye would have believed Me ; for he wrote of
Me. But if ye believe not his writings, how shall ye

believe My words ?' (John v. 46, 47). The traditions with which the Pharisees overlaid the laws and teachings of Moses He branded as making the word of God of no effect (Mark vii. 13). But the *writings* of Moses, unadulterated by tradition, were worthy of the confidence which the people placed in them. *Their* authority rested on the fact that they *were* the writings of Moses, the servant of God. And if Christ did not so believe, He was seeking support for His claims in a popular fallacy, a popular misbelief—this, viz., that it was Moses, whom the people reverenced as possessed of Divine authority, that had written those things concerning Him which He found in the earlier books in the Old Testament. We have here something very different from a mere casual or incidental quotation of an ancient book by the name of its reputed author. We have a solemn argument and remonstrance based on His and the people's belief in the Mosaic authorship ; in fact, an unqualified testimony to Moses as a prophet, a lawgiver, and a writer. To the spirit of this appeal we have a very solemn confirmation in the parable of the rich man and Lazarus. The rich man appeals to Abraham on behalf of his brothers, and Abraham says to him, 'They have Moses and the prophets ; let them hear them. If they hear not Moses and the prophets, neither will they be persuaded, though one rose from the dead' (Luke xvi. 29, 31).

In the matter of Christ's testimony we cannot overlook the fact that He associated the name of Moses expressly with scriptures which are now declared not to have been his. For example, to a leper whom He had healed He said, 'Go thy way, shew thyself to the priest, and offer the gift that Moses commanded' (Matt. viii. 4). Now the command of Moses is to be found in the very heart of that priestly code which the critics say was framed centuries after the days of Moses. The law concerning leprosy occupies two long chapters in the Book of Leviticus, the thirteenth and fourteenth. It is prefaced thus : ' The Lord spake unto Moses and Aaron, saying ;' and this preface is not peculiar to the law of leprosy.   It would be only the ' foolishness ' of argument to limit the testimony of Christ to the one law to which He had occasion to refer when He instructed the healed man to do what Moses had commanded.   Immediately before and immediately after this law, we have other laws introduced in the same words.   And if the one came from Moses, so did the others.

We find Christ associating Moses personally with incidents to which He referred, as in Luke xx. 37 and John iii. 14.   And it is worthy of notice how He distinguished the part which belonged to Moses and the part which did not, in matters with which he was connected.   Thus, referring to circumcision, He reminded the Jews that it did not originate in a law of Moses, Moses having to do only with the day on which the rite was to be performed (John vii. 21, 22 ; Lev. xii. 3).   And as to the law of marriage, the part which prescribed the giving of a bill to a divorced woman alone belonged to Moses (Matt. xix. 7 ; Deut. xxiv. 1). One of the laws which Christ thus ascribed to Moses is found in the Levitical or priestly code, and the other in the book which they say was written hundreds of years after his time.

The reader of the Gospels cannot fail to receive the impression that in all Christ's conversation with the Jews, our Lord regarded Moses not as a mere title by which certain books were known, but as personally the actor in the history which they record, and the author of the legislation which they contain : ' Did not Moses give you the law (Christ said), and yet none of you keepeth the law ? ' (John vii. 19). ' We are Moses' disciples (the Jews said to the man to whom Christ had given sight). We know that God spake unto Moses : as for this man, we know not whence he is ' (John ix. 28, 29, R. V.).

This faith in Moses, as the responsible author of the books which bear his name, was inherited by Christ's disciples. The apostle John says expressly, ' The law was given by Moses ' (John i. 17). And the apostle Paul specifies the very date at which Moses gave the law. It was four hundred and thirty years after the great promise of blessing and grace to mankind was given to Abraham (Gal. iii. 17). In fulfilling their mission ' to the Jew first,' the apostles invariably appealed to Moses and the prophets. ' Moses,' James reminded his brethren (Acts xv. 21), ' of old time hath in every city them that preach him, being read in the synagogues every

Sabbath day.' And in every synagogue to which the apostles had access their concern was to show out of the Scriptures that Jesus was the Christ. In doing this they began, as Christ Himself had done, with Moses. If the scriptures of Moses were not genuinely his, the apostles were either deceivers or deceived. And if the Messiahship of Jesus of Nazareth could not bear an appeal to Moses and the prophets, the Jews were entitled to reject Him.

What shall we say to all this—what that can throw doubt on, or minimize, what seems at least to be conclusive evidence that our Old Testament comes to us with, to use a modern phrase, the imprimatur of the Son of God Himself? Some have a vague impression that the testimony of Christ will be materially modified when judged in the light of the apostolic words now translated thus: 'Who, being in the form of God, counted it not a prize to be on an equality with God, but emptied Himself, taking the form of a servant' (Phil. ii. 6, 7); but is it so? Kenotic theories which are offered to us to explain the inner meaning, the essential contents, of the words 'He emptied Himself,' all leave us unsatisfied and with a feeling that the mystery of the Incarnation and of its effect on the condition of the Incarnate One must remain a mystery. From all attempts at abstract definition we turn aside to the concrete history of the Son of God in the days of His flesh as we have it in the Gospels. What that history tells us on the subject we are now considering is too plain to be mistaken. And reverent expounders of Kenotic theories themselves do not hesitate to say that, whatever amount of truth may be in them, it is certain that not only was Jesus Christ an infallible Teacher, but that He was 'incapable of misleading.'

If we are asked whether Jesus Christ Himself did not confess to a limitation of knowledge, we reply that He did on one occasion and as to one thing: 'Of that day and that hour knoweth no man, no, not the angels which are in heaven, neither the Son, but the Father' (Mark xiii. 32). The proper inference from these words is, not that there might be many other things which He did not know, but that if there were other things which He did not know, He would have made the like confession instead of this. We find Him actually claiming a knowledge far more wonderful than that which He disclaimed: 'All things are delivered unto Me of My Father: and no man knoweth the Son, but the Father; neither knoweth any man the Father, save the Son, and he to whomsoever the Son will reveal Him' (Matt. xi. 27). The 'all things' delivered to Christ by the Father are explained in part at least by words used on other occasions—'All power,' 'all judgement,' the forgiving of sin, and the giving of life. Need we wonder that the apostle Peter should say to Him, 'Lord, Thou knowest all things' (John xxi. 17)? The apostle might be puzzled by metaphysical questions as to omniscience.

And yet he would not withdraw his words. He had seen enough and heard enough practically to anticipate the claim which Christ asserted for Himself to John in Patmos : 'I am He which searcheth the reins and hearts' (Rev. ii. 23). Christ had often detected the unspoken thoughts of His disciples and of the scribes. He discerned from the beginning the heart of Judas, and knew that he would betray Him. He prophesied the denial of Peter ; He foretold His own death and the manner of it, His resurrection on the third day, and His ascension ; He foretold the siege and destruction of Jerusalem, and He foretold what is yet future to us, and is therefore still unaccomplished. 'If in all this and much more there was not displayed (as Canon Rawlinson says) a Divine consciousness, knowledge more than human, it is difficult to see how such knowledge could have been manifested '—knowledge, be it observed, which was His while in that state which is described and covered by the apostolic words, 'He emptied Himself, and took upon Him the form of a servant.'

It seems almost trifling with a great and sacred subject to suggest that Christ might have chosen to be ignorant, or to pass by, as unworthy of notice, so unimportant a matter as the authorship of certain books. With all reverence we may say that He could not have so chosen. And we have evidence that He did not so choose. There is no element of reality in the favourite formula, 'critical and literary questions' which might have been left to later ages, that was not included in our Lord's averment touching the 'writings of Moses.' At the risk of some repetition let me say, in the words of Professor Cheyne, that Christ could not have mistaken the meaning of His own Bible. The profoundest critical and exegetical question which had to be solved was the true meaning of ancient prophecy. Christ solved it ; and His argument with the Jews involved the solution of the further critical and literary question, who wrote certain books in which prophecy respecting Him was found ? *He said it was Moses.* The authorship was an essential part of His argument.

THIRDLY : **The reverent and believing Bible reader may well recoil from the processes of the Higher Criticism because of their moral implications and bearings.**

No wider gulf can be found or imagined between the ordinary reader, whose spiritual senses have been exercised to discern good and evil in the matter of honesty and truthfulness, and the criticism which necessitates a charge of untruthfulness and imposture against the writers of large portions of the Old Testament. I am well aware that there are critics who deny that this charge lies fairly against their theories. They repudiate the word forgery, and imagine what they would call scientific explanations of what to the common mind looks very like forgery. But the common mind recoils from the special pleading which their case needs, and is disposed to apply to it the words of the prophet, slightly altered for the occasion, 'Though thou wash thee with nitre, and take thee much soap, yet thine iniquity cannot be washed away.' Let any reader, common or uncommon, read without note or comment, the twenty-second chapter of 2 Kings and the thirty-fourth of 2 Chronicles. He can judge of their meaning as well as the most learned scholar. When the temple is being repaired in the days of good King Josiah, a book is found, which in Kings is called 'the book of the law,' and in Chronicles, 'a book of the law of the Lord given by the hand of Moses.' Hilkiah the high priest, who found it, sends it by Shaphan the scribe to the king, who, on reading it or some portion of it, sends the high priest and some others 'to enquire of the Lord concerning the words of the book.' They go to Huldah the prophetess, and 'commune with her' on the subject, and she confirms the threatenings of the book because 'Their *fathers* had not kept the word of the Lord, to do after all that was written in this book.'

All this seems very plain. The book that was found was 'the book of the law which was given by Moses.' Even if it was called, as in Kings, only 'the book of the law,' nothing else could be meant than that it was the book of the law of Moses. The '*fathers*' had had this book in their possession, for their sin was that 'they had not kept the word of the Lord, to do after all that was written in this book' (2 Chron.

xxxiv. 21). This was the understanding of the high priest, the scribe, the prophetess, and the king. *Or they pretended that it was.* The critical theory is that the book was what is known to us as the Book of Deuteronomy, and that it was written, not in the days of Moses, but now, in the days of Josiah, to aid Josiah in the reformation on which his heart was set. Dr. Driver prefers to think that it was written in the days of Manasseh, Josiah's grandfather. But this makes no difference in the moral character of the transaction. Whoever wrote it in either reign was guilty of a fraud. If the finder of the book was not himself the author of the book, he was easily imposed on—that he should accept as by Moses, containing laws and threatenings which professed to be of Moses, a book which the '*fathers*' had never seen, a book against which the fathers, not having seen it, had not sinned. One wonders too at the simplicity of the idolatrous multitude and their idolatrous leaders, that they should be frightened out of their evil but much-loved ways, by threatenings of judgement, which, they could easily prove, had not been heard of till some unknown contemporary had falsely put on them the seal of Moses !

The glosses which are put on this supposed transaction to hide its nakedness may be set aside, in view of the boldness, one might say the nonchalance, with which the critics ignore the plainest and most unmistakable historic statements of the book, and substitute for them their own subjective impressions. Take an example. The great song, worthy even of the great

Moses, and which is associated with the 'song of the Lamb' in Rev. xv, which occupies the thirty-second chapter of the Book of Deuteronomy, is prefaced thus: 'Moses spake in the ears of all the congregation of Israel the words of this song, until they were ended.' The prophetic forecasts of the future of the tribes which we find in the thirty-third chapter are prefaced thus: 'This is the blessing, wherewith Moses the man of God blessed the children of Israel before his death.' But these positive and specific averments are as if they were not—of no account in the way of Dr. Driver's criticism. He will judge for himself when and by whom this 'song' and this 'blessing' were written. And his judgement is this: 'The song shows great originality in form, being a presentation of prophetical thoughts in a poetical dress, which is unique in the Old Testament. The standpoint, whether assumed or real, from which the poet speaks is subsequent to the Mosaic age, to which (in vv. 7–12) he looks back as to a distant past. The theme is developed with great literary and artistic skill; the images are varied and expressive; the parallelism is usually regular and very forcible.' Dr. Driver's only doubt is whether the song is by the same hand as the body of the book. The internal evidence, he thinks, does not absolutely preclude its being by the same author, but 'the contents hardly leave it a possibility.'

I am not concerned to reply to this criticism. Only I may remark that it is rather strange that the 'great literary and artistic skill' of the unknown author

of this composition did not save him from putting into
the mouth of Moses words, in which Dr. Driver discovers an anachronism which proves it to have been
written 'after the Mosaic age'—a great blunder surely
on the part of so skilled a writer. My object is to
show how the Higher Critical theory of the book
necessitates the admission of untruthfulness at every
point. The book may say that a certain composition,
full of solemn truth and admonition (xxxii. 44–47), was
written—all the words of it to the end (xxxi. 30)—by
Moses. No, says the critic ; this is to be ascribed to
the literary skill and art of the author, unless indeed
it was interpolated by some 'redactor' who found the
song somewhere and tacked it on to the book. From
such methods of interpretation the reverent reader
recoils with the conviction that if the Old Testament
is true, the theory is an offence to both the intellect
and the conscience of its trustful readers.

But if we would have an adequate sense of the
extent of untruthfulness and deception of which
the Book of Deuteronomy is guilty according to the
'critical theory' so called, we must read the book
from beginning to end, and pause over its many
averments respecting its own contents, and compare
them with the averments or implications of the theory
which denies the Mosaic authorship. The very first
sentences of the book are these : ' These be the
words which Moses spake unto all Israel on this side
Jordan in the wilderness, in the plain over against

the Red Sea, between Paran, and Tophel, and
Laban, and Hazeroth, and Dizahab. (There are eleven
days' journey from Horeb by the way of Mount Seir
unto Kadesh-barnea.)   And it came to pass in the
fortieth year, in the eleventh month, on the first day
of the month, that Moses spake unto the children
of Israel, according unto all that the Lord had given
him in commandment unto them ; after he had slain
Sihon the king of the Amorites, which dwelt in
Heshbon, and Og the king of Bashan, which dwelt
at Astaroth in Edrei: on this side Jordan, in the
land of Moab, began Moses to declare this law, saying,
The Lord our God spake unto us in Horeb, saying'—
and so on.

If it be true that the book was written in the days
of Josiah, nine hundred years or thereabouts after
Israel entered Canaan, or possibly somewhat earlier,
in the days of Josiah's grandfather, and that the
addresses to the people which it puts into the lips
of Moses were manufactured for a purpose by some
unknown genius nearly a millennium after the days
of Moses ; and, moreover, that the incidents and
circumstances which introduce these speeches, and
the recital of principal events which are said to have
occurred during the forty years in the wilderness which
occupy the earlier chapters of the book, are not
real, except so far as vague traditions which may
have survived for nearly a thousand years may have
suggested them—not real, but imagined and invented
to give plausibility to the speeches—how shall we

characterize the book's own description of its contents?
How would a judge in a court of law describe it?
Would he hesitate to say that if the true history of
the book be what certain critics allege, the preface
to the book is nothing short of a lie? He would
scarcely have patience to listen to explanations or
apologies. Let him read the book for himself, and
he will tell the men at his bar that the lie which is
told on the frontispiece of the book pervades it from
the beginning to the end. Not a lie—the apologist
the special pleader, will say—the book is constructed
after the manner of classical historians, 'who put
fictitious discourses into the mouths of their principal
characters, not with any intention to deceive, but
simply for the purpose of throwing light on the historical situation.' But in this instance is it not of the
very essence of the critical theory, that it was the
object of the writer or writers to make the people of
the days of Manasseh or of Josiah believe that Moses
had spoken the words which they put into his mouth—
to give these words greater authority than they would
otherwise have, as a protest against idolatry and as
a plea for the worship of Jehovah? The ascription of
the words which we find in the book to Moses, was,
on this showing, a bold conscious falsehood ; and the
writers took every precaution to prevent its fictitious
character from being discovered. They specified
the very year, the very month, the very day of the
month, on which they said Moses began to speak
what the book records (Deut. i. 3). And to make

their readers feel quite sure that they had the very words of Moses in the book and no others, they represented him as saying, ' Ye shall not add unto the word which I command you, neither shall ye diminish ought from it, that ye may keep the commandments of the Lord your God which I command you' (ch. iv. 2).

Nothing can save the writers of this book, if they were, as the critical theory says they were, men of the days of Manasseh or Josiah, from the charge of conscious and painstaking forgery. This, every one feels, is an ugly word. But all its ugliness and consequences must be faced by the learned men who deny the book's own statement of its origin and character.

Colonel Conder has no hesitation in saying, 'We have no knowledge of a Jewish scholar mutilating the writings of his ancestors, or of his composing a book of fragments from unacknowledged sources, linked together by a few words of his own writing. That kind of bookmaking is characteristic rather of our own times; and no editor who so presented to us, as the law written by Moses, a composite later forgery could escape the charge of literary dishonesty' (*The Bible and the East*, p. 90).

As to the examples of classical historians to which we are referred, who put speeches into the mouths of their characters, 'not to deceive, but to throw light on the historical situation,' when we turn to Deuteronomy we find the speeches not throwing light on the historical situation, but the historical situation throwing light on the speeches. The speeches grow

out of the occasions and incidents which the book
records, and if either be unhistorical, the other must
be likewise. 'To most of us,' says Principal Douglas,
'a remarkable voucher for the truth of the book is the
interlacing of the history and the legislation throughout
the whole Pentateuch, so that we feel the utmost
difficulty in conceiving how the one should have
come into existence without the other' (*Lex Mosaica,*
p. 59).

The Book of Leviticus shares the fate of the Book
of Deuteronomy in the hands of the Higher Critic.
Some of its ordinances, he admits, may be based on
practices which had somehow already come into
existence, but these practices were not based on
any Mosaic law. That there is not the shadow of
historical authority for implicating Ezekiel and Ezra
or any of their contemporaries in the creation of the
priestly code, is patent on the face of the books
which bear these honoured names. Let it be remem-
bered that the most advanced scholarship has no
advantage over the non-expert in forming a judgement
on this matter, and that the non-expert is quite
capable of appreciating the general grounds on which
the Mosaic authorship of Leviticus may be maintained, as these are stated by Canon Rawlinson thus :
(1) 'The Levitical code is such a law as Moses, from
his position and the circumstances of his time, might
have been expected to promulgate ; (2) That it is
such a law as the later history of the people of Israel

postulates and requires; (3) That the human testimony
to the fact of Moses having given this law is amply
sufficient to establish it, being extraordinarily full and
varied; and (4) That the fact rests not merely, as
most facts, on human evidence, but also on a witness
who is Divine' (*Lex Mosaica*, p. 21).

Our present argument, however, has to do only
with the moral implication of the critical theory.
Opening the book and reading from beginning to end,
we find that all its ordinances and precepts are
prefaced by the solemn words, 'The Lord spake
unto Moses.' These words occur some thirty times
in the book; these thirty assertions are, according
to the theory, thirty falsehoods, and these thirty falsehoods and others of their kind in other books were—
one hesitates to write it even hypothetically—written
deliberately by holy men, unknown worthies, to
create and exalt an order of priests which had not
existed before at least by Divine authority; and, it
may be (sanctifying the lower motive by a higher)
at the same time, the better to secure obedience to
the Divine will. The supposition is so gross that
it may be rejected at once, not without some indigna-
tion, by the moral sense of Bible readers.

One other instance, incidentally referred to already, in which the non-expert reader is struck with
the boldness with which criticism deals with plain
historic statements, and practically treats them as
untrue. In the story of the re-establishment of the

Jews in their own land after their exile in Babylon,
we read how that Ezra read to great assemblies, day
by day, out of a book the language of which now
needed to be translated or interpreted to the people.
That book is called again and again ' The Book of
the law of Moses, the man of God ' (comp. Ezra vii. 6 ;
Neh. viii. 1, 9, 14 ; x. 29). While yet in exile Ezra
was held in high repute, not as a lawgiver, but ' as
a *scribe* of the law of the God of Heaven.' His com-
mission from the Persian monarch describes him as
' the priest, the scribe, even a scribe of the words of
the commandments of Jehovah, and of His statutes
to Israel ' (Ezra vii. 11). And he had authority not to
form a new constitution for Israel, but to restore the
old : ' Thou art sent to inquire concerning Judah
and Jerusalem, according to the law of thy God
which is in thine hand ' (Ezra vii. 14, 21, 26). He was
apparently the great-grandson of Seraiah, the chief
priest of the beginning of the exile (2 Kings xxv.
18 ; Ezra vii. 1–5). That the law which he had in his
hand was the law of Moses which his grandfather or
great-grandfather had carried with him to Babylon,
can scarcely be called a supposition, it is so obviously
natural and inevitable, for on no other supposition
could he regard the book of which he was so earnest
a student in the days of his exile (vii. 10) as the book
of the law whose ' statutes and judgements ' the
Lord had given by Moses, and which he was now
ambitious to teach to his people. Such a man,
prepared both by education and by personal zeal

E

for the great task of the religious restoration of
Israel, could not be beguiled either through ignorance
or through carelessness, into the adoption, as of
Moses, of 'statutes and judgements,' not a century
old ; and into the absorption or interpolation of them
into the body of the ancient book which contained
the statutes and judgements which were really Mosaic.
But the honour of Ezra and the honour of the history
must not stand in the way of theory. Deceived or
deceiver, the book which the great scribe, according
to the theory, read to his assembled countrymen,
was in no proper sense the book of the commandments of the Lord and of His statutes to Israel *by
the hand of Moses.* Here, however, the critic and
the history are irreconcileable—the history knowing
nothing of a priestly code which received its 'final
touches' from the hand of Ezra.

There are critics who take no pains to explain
away the conclusion that the critical theory leaves
the authors of the historical books of the Old
Testament chargeable with dishonesty, and in fact
that the books are gangrened with fraud. Kuenen,
for example, says that the authors of the books from
Genesis to Esther 'fearlessly allowed themselves to be
guided in their statements by the wants of the present
and the requirements of the future. *They considered
themselves exempt from all responsibility,'* and as to
the Books of Chronicles, the priests coloured or
invented the history to suit their ends without
regard to truth.

But 'here (as has been well said) endless difficulties arise to the critics. The books of Moses are so high in moral sentiment, so pure in moral principle, so strong in defence of righteousness, and so full of reverence for truth and God, that it is impossible, morally, to believe that men so falsifying history for a purpose could at the same time have composed such a noble moral structure as the Pentateuch [1].' To which we may add that the history of literature cannot furnish a parallel to the intellectual achievement of the man who could create the Pentateuch out of his own brain, and a few floating national traditions seven or eight centuries after the period and the (supposed) events which it narrates, and give the whole such an air of verisimilitude as to deceive or at least mislead all after ages. The genius, not Isaiah, to whom criticism ascribes the last twenty-seven chapters of the book which bears the name of Isaiah, is not to be compared to him. And yet the moral sense of this great genius was so perverse that he did not hesitate to say times without number, that God spoke words which He did not speak, and ordained laws which He did not ordain !

Non-experts, the unlearned, are in a position to pronounce an unhesitating verdict on the subject of this chapter.

[1] Dr. Alexander Stewart, of Aberdeen University.

FOURTHLY : **The Bible reader does not find in new theories, what he has a right to demand, an intelligent and sufficient substitute for that which they would displace.**

The non-experts whose cause I am pleading have reason to distrust and reject the new theory of Hebrew scripture and Hebrew history, because it fails to supply an intelligible and consistent substitute for the old. It is no small matter, looking at it merely from a literary point of view, to pronounce condemnation on that old, which has come to us bearing the seal of a great nation whose self-esteem it never flattered, whose misdeeds it unsparingly condemned, unbroken through more centuries than any other nation, any Western nation at least, has lived. Join in such condemnation, and you are bound to give us a theory of the books and of the history which will recognize acknowledged facts and adequately explain them. On Christian and other grounds we consider ourselves entitled, as we have argued, to reject any theory which involves a charge of historical dishonesty against the Hebrew books. But passing from this, and this aspect of the new criticism, we demand a theory, the fruit, let it be, of the freest manipulation of known materials and the freest use of the critic's imagination, that shall be intelligible and consistent, and that shall supply a credible explanation of the books.

The critics begin with cutting up Genesis and portions of the other books of the Pentateuch, with

the history interspersed, into bits, and these bits they
designate with letters which remind one of an algebraic
problem. The process began modestly with A, B,
C, D. But it grew till we have J. E. Q. P.—with
J^1 and J^2, E^1 and E^2, P^1 and P^2 and P^3, D^1 and D^2,
which represent different strata in the hypothetic
original documents. Different redactors are embraced
under the general symbol R, Rj, who combined
J and E, R^d, who added D to J E, and Rh, who completed the Hexateuch (Pentateuch and Joshua) by
combining P with J. E. D. The bits, as I call them,
thus designated and stamped, written six, eight, and
ten centuries after the Exodus, are said to be the
primary sources of patriarchal and Mosaic history!
If so, the result must have been accomplished by
some such mighty and beneficent power as that
which transformed the primeval chaos into kosmos.
Readers who do not possess the critical 'second
sight' are more likely to conclude that having
kosmos already in the Hebrew books, criticism has
toiled to convert it into chaos. We ask with confidence whether the process alleged by the critics,
or anything like it, can be made intelligible to any
but the critics themselves? And it may be fairly
asked whether it is intelligible even to them?

Then as to consistency. The documents, thus
discovered and separated, are further discovered to
be at variance with each other in their statements
respecting numerous particulars, thus invalidating
each other's testimony; and besides they are very

incomplete. Numerous gaps and omissions occur in each. 'But what is more serious,' as Dr. W. H. Green says, 'the parts that yet remain have been manipulated by the various redactors. The order of events has been disturbed, events really distinct have been confused and mistaken for one and the same—while statements which are misleading have been inserted with the view of harmonizing what cannot be reconciled'—and so on, so on.

We look in vain for consistency in this process, or in any result which it could possibly effect. Nor are we aided in the least, rather are we further confounded by the hypotheses which have followed one after another to meet fresh difficulties as they have arisen—and which are known by many names, some of them high-sounding—such as Fragment Hypothesis, Document Hypothesis, Supplement Hypothesis, Crystallization Hypothesis, Modified Document Hypothesis, and Development Hypothesis. There is no subject that gives more scope both for sarcasm and for sound argument than the history of these hypotheses, and the irreconcileable differences which separate critic from critic, and many times the critic from himself at different stages of his mental development. But we forbear.

There is a short and easy method by which imagination can account for the unity and self-consistency, the homogeneity and naturalness, of 'the marvellous' books which we call the 'Pentateuch,' but it does not find favour with English critics. We owe it to what

may be called the French school. Give up all attempt
to determine what measure of historic truth, if any,
can be found in the books of the Old Testament.
These books, with one or two unimportant exceptions,
had no existence in the ages to which they relate.
They are the product of creative genius, in the age
which saw the disappearance of the Persian Empire,
'when the Empire of Alexander moulded the minds
of thinking men in a universalist's mould.' To the
creative genius of that age we owe all the prophetic
and historical books. 'Their narratives have not even
an historical residuum, but are simply illustrative
religious lessons, which bring in all the patriarchs,
Moses, Elijah, and so on. Old names, Egypt and
Assyria and Babylon, are used in the prophecies
to represent those successors of Alexander the Great
who oppressed the Jews.'

One cannot help admiring the simplicity of this
theory. Sweeping away the entire old fabric, leaving
not one stone upon another, it builds afresh on ground
not even cumbered with ruins, and, building at its own
sweet pleasure, it can give symmetry and harmony to
its new structure. But this theory is too advanced
and radical even for the boldest of the theorists with
whom we have most to do. They, to use the words
of Principal Douglas, reject these teachings as wild
fancies. 'I agree with them,' he adds, 'only I do not
think these fancies essentially wilder than their own.
And Vernes and his friends present a view of the
construction of our Old Testament which, apart from

its want of all historical foundation, is much more attractive and perhaps even less burdened with difficulties than theirs.'

The vagaries of criticism can boast both of age and of novelty. Some twenty years ago, or nearly, there appeared a book entitled *Peregrinus Proteus*, by J. M. Cotterill of Edinburgh, in which the author laboured, with no small learning, to prove that not a few ancient works, including Clement's famous Letter to the Corinthians, which have hitherto been regarded as genuine, were forgeries, 'the natural productions' of the age of the revival of letters, an 'age of fraud,' and that the fabricator of the books was in all probability no less a man than the famous French printer, Henry Stephens, known as a Protestant and a fervent denouncer of deceit and superstition, who died in 1520. A contemporary critic of Mr. Cotterill's book said that his method of getting rid of historical evidence reminded him of nothing so much as of Cardinal Manning's famous saying, that we must be delivered from history by the infallible dicta of the Church. It is paralleled now by the 'infallible dicta' of a very fallible Higher Criticism.

FIFTHLY: **The faith of the Bible reader in the histories of the Old Testament, and in the account which they give of themselves, is strengthened by the fact that they are confirmed, and that in a very remarkable manner, by modern archaeological discoveries.**

There is one department of inquiry which is accessible to all thoughtful students of Holy Scripture, and in which mere scholarship, Hebrew or Classical, gives critics no advantage over those who do not possess it. It is that which is concerned with the results of modern archaeological discoveries in Assyria, Palestine, and Egypt. The most modern living experts in this matter, known to England, are such as Boscawen, Sayce, and Lieut.-Col. Conder, and their testimony confirms and greatly expands the conclusions which defenders of the truth of Bible history had already reached with less knowledge of the facts. It almost looks as if not 'the stars' but a more real power was now fighting conclusively against the assailants of the Bible. Plausible objections to which believers felt that they could offer a sufficient answer, though not an answer that rendered doubt impossible, are now proved, I may say demonstrated, to be utterly groundless. And while these are negatived, positive confirmations of Bible history, the patriarchal and later, as striking as they were unexpected, are furnished by recent discovery. Many pages might be filled with illustrations of this averment. But I content myself with a few general statements.

Even with reference to the Book of Genesis Col. Conder does not hesitate to say that the tradition of early times which it has preserved is proved correct by the results of monumental study. 'Viewed in the light of extant monuments,' he says, 'the story of Genesis presents to us a true picture of the state of

Asia before the great Egyptian conquests of the sixteenth century B.C.' Prof. Sayce writes to the same effect : 'The narratives which the Higher Criticism had pronounced to be the unhistorical fragments of popular tradition are being shown by archaeological discovery to be historical after all. Contemporaneous monuments are continually coming to light which prove that in the story of the Patriarchs [in Genesis] and of the Exodus we have truth and not legend . . . . . . Year by year, almost month by month, fresh discoveries are breaking in upon us, each more marvellous than the last, but all as regards the Pentateuch in favour of the Old rather than the New.' 'It may come to be recognized,' says Col. Conder, 'that the words of the Pentateuch form a better foundation for history than the fragments of Manetho, or the baseless theories of those who set aside its dates and its geography as fabrications of a later priesthood.'

Of Joshua he says, 'On no book of the Bible has recent exploration cast more light than on that relating to the story of the Hebrew conquest of Canaan.' Of all recent discoveries, perhaps the most remarkable is that of letters sent to Egypt by the Amorite king of Jerusalem. 'They show,' says Col. Conder, 'that the Abiri [the Hebrews] came from Seir, and fought at Ajalon ; that they invaded the Philistine plains, and destroyed all the Canaanite rulers. Their notices agree exactly with the Bible account of Joshua's first campaign. The principal passages in the Jerusalem letters clearly

indicate the path of conquest.' 'The tone of all
the Canaanite letters is a despairing cry for help to
Egypt; but none of them record that any help was
sent, though eagerly expected' (*The Bible and the
East*, pp. 103–113).

The most *far-reaching* discovery of recent archae-
ology is probably that which has swept away for ever
an allegation which was long boastfully used as an
argument to prove that the writing of the Pentateuch
by Moses or by any Israelite in his age was an impossibility. 'It was tacitly assumed that the literary
use of writing could not have been known to an
Israelite in the time of Moses, and consequently that
none of the narratives in the Pentateuch can go back
to so early a period. They must all belong, it was
urged, to a later age, when little authentic record was
preserved of the Mosaic days, and when the imagination of the author or his contemporaries had to supply
the missing facts.' There could be, it was alleged,
no written contemporaneous evidence of the events
of patriarchal times narrated in Genesis, so that the
history of any of these events could not be trusted.
If, for example, there was no one to record the meeting
of Melchizedek and Abram or the conquest of Palestine
by the kings of Aram Naharaim, the critic was justified
in disputing the historical credibility of these tales.
'Unrecorded events soon pass into forgetfulness or
become enveloped in an atmosphere of myth and
romance.'

'But now a lost world of culture and civilization

has been brought to light first in Egypt, then in Assyria and Babylonia, and finally in the lands of the Eastern Mediterranean.' 'We can now study the letters of Canaanites who lived before the days of Moses.' The Tell-el-Amarna tablets tell us that in the century before Exodus Palestine was a land of books and schools. All over Canaan there was an active correspondence going on even in a foreign tongue. Such a fact implies an abundance of schools and teachers and pupils. As in Babylon and Assyria, so too in Canaan, there must have been libraries in which the clay books with their wedge-like letters were stored and studied. The historian who desired to compile a history of the cities of Canaan would have had at his disposal more than enough of con-temporaneous material. From a period earlier than that of Abraham there were documents containing history of the most authentic and trustworthy kind. The assumption that the Israelites who escaped from Egypt and invaded Canaan were a horde of illiterate barbarians is one which cannot be maintained. To admit that the Israelites were once in Egypt, and yet to deny to them a knowledge at the time they fled from it, is certainly not consonant with the principles of probability and common-sense.

These sentences culled, for the sake of brevity, from Professor Sayce, without the details amid which we find them, justify the general statements which have been already quoted from Sayce and Conder respecting the Book of Genesis. This book, it is obvious, occupies a different position from that of the other books of the Pentateuch, inasmuch as its contents are pre-Mosaic. It was the first battle-ground of criticism. But all that needs to be said about it here is, that, apart from the witness of Christ to its facts, all improbability arising from the nature and the date of these facts, at least the greater part of these facts, is now more than neutralized. There is internal evidence in the book that it is not a mere compilation of documents or documentary fragments that have come from one knows not how many sources, but that it is written on a distinctly careful plan. Of this there is patent sign in the heading or introduction to ten consecutive sections of the book—' These are the generations,' in ii. 4 ; v. 1 ; vi. 9 ; x. 1 ; xi. 10 ; xi. 27 ; xxv. 12 ; xxv. 19; xxxvi. 1 ; xxxvii. 2. For the greater part of these there need have been no lack of written materials. But the use of these materials in the preparation of the history does not render the book less a book of Moses, than it would have been if it had contained only speculations woven out of his own brain. And it is not too much to say that the materials were welded together by a wisdom more than that of man, a wisdom which could foresee and contemplate the future.

Well may the believer in Bible history congratulate himself, and expect with confidence the unearthing of more witness to the truth of the old story.

SIXTHLY: **The non-expert, instead of being reconciled to the newer criticism, is repelled from it, by the avowal on the part of the critics of faith in the inspiration of the Jewish Scrip-tures.**

The critics do not deny, rather they maintain, they say, the inspiration of Scripture, *but*, 'the current doctrine of Scripture and of Divine inspiration requires revision.' Be it so—and, making no account of such critics as Kuenen and Wellhausen, to whom supernatural revelation is non-existent—what revision, of what amount and of what kind, will bring the doctrine of Divine inspiration into harmony with the facts *as understood by the critics*? We can find no answer to this question in old familiar discussions respecting verbal inspiration and the mode of inspira-tion. We must even go beyond the question of 'the strict inerrancy of Scripture, of absolute accuracy in unimportant minutiae, or precision in matters of science.' 'The question is whether any dependence can be placed on the historical truth of the Bible; whether our confidence in the facts recorded in the Pen-tateuch and in other books rests upon any really trust-worthy basis; facts, be it observed, not of mere scientific or antiquarian interest, but which mark the course of God's revelations to the Patriarchs and to Moses.' But this is not all. It is a fundamental assumption of critics that the redactors to whom they ascribe the present condition of the books misunderstood or mis-

represented their sources—the more ancient fragments
or portions on which they operated; 'that narratives,
which were but varying accounts of the same thing,
were supposed by them to relate to distinct occurrences,
and they have treated them as such, wrongly assigning
them to different occasions and perhaps different
persons; that they have combined their sources in
such a way as to give a wrong colouring to their
contents, so that they make a false impression and
convey a meaning quite different from that which
properly belonged to them in their original connexion.
And the chief value and interest of the critic is thought
to be the new light which he brings into the narrative
and the altered meaning which he discovers by undoing
the work of the redactors, who are supposed to have
cut away much precious material from their documents
that is now irrecoverably lost, and to have modified
the mutilated remnant which they have handed down
to us' (Green, *Higher Criticism of the Pentateuch*,
163, 170).

Now where in all this do we find 'the place of
inspiration'? In the documents or fragments of documents which are supposed to have been the 'original
sources'? On the critical hypothesis, no one knows
what they were or whence they came—only this is
known, that is, to the critics, that they were confused,
mutually contradictory, and liable to all manner of
misunderstanding. The redactors cannot have
believed such documents to have been inspired,
—or if they had, would they have dared to treat them

as they did ?   Shall we find 'the place' of inspiration
in the redactors themselves ?   Waiving the fact that
these editors, who in successive generations have
moulded the book into its present form, belong to the
race of the great Unknowns of literature, their work
is as unreliable, according to the critics, as was the
condition of the materials on which they operated.
They misunderstood or misrepresented their sources,
and, according to the critics to whom alone we owe
our knowledge of their existence, they combined their
sources in such a way as to give a wrong colouring
to their contents.

Were they inspired in doing this ?   We read of bring-
ing a clean thing out of an unclean, but that were an
easy process compared with that which we are asked to
accept when we are told that the book, as we have
it, is the completed product of documents which even
in their first estate were either self-contradictory or
unintelligible, and of the toils of editors who misunderstood the documents, and blundered in piecing them
together or in framing narratives out of them ; and
thus written it is inspired !   Verily our 'doctrine of
inspiration' must be 'revised' in order to meet the
exigency to which we are now reduced.   We have
still to go in search of 'the place' of inspiration, and
if it is to be found anywhere it must be in the critics
themselves.   Their predecessors, the redactors, have
erred, and their work is not satisfactory.   They, now
sitting on the throne of judgement, tell us the whole
truth and nothing but the truth.   If we deny their

claim to authority or to the inspiration which justifies authority, they can produce a precedent from a most venerable source. In the Council of Trent the question was earnestly discussed whether the Vulgate translation of the Scriptures was inspired. There was reasonable likelihood, it was argued, that the Spirit who had dictated the original had also dictated the translation. Nay, it was ingeniously argued, says Mr. Froude, that the Council then sitting was confessedly inspired. The Council therefore had but to approve the Vulgate, and the Vulgate itself would be inspired!

Very logical! Quite a precedent for the critics. They have only to assert their own inspiration, and then all else over which they throw the mantle of their authority becomes inspired in virtue of theirs. In this we have the ultimate ' Revision ' of the doctrine of Inspiration!

But the non-expert cannot receive it. It is too hard a saying for both his reason and his conscience. Accepting as he does, and that on grounds which satisfy both reason and conscience, the Old Testament as a record of Divine Revelations given at sundry times and in divers manners, the reverent believer revolts, as I have maintained, from all theories which imply any approach to dishonesty or fraud in the record. With equal vehemence, I might say with equal loathing, he revolts from any theory which would convert the unholy into the holy by putting on it the seal of God, the seal of what apostles held to be the Inspiration of the Holy Ghost (2 Pet. i. 21 ; 2 Tim. iii. 16).

F

SEVENTHLY: **Any argument which may be drawn from the plausibilities of criticism is easily rebutted by the fact that the same sort of criticism, applied to any ancient or even modern book, might be made to yield similar results.**

The remark is often made, and made with truth, that the processes by which the Higher Criticism disintegrates the books of the Old Testament, might be applied with equal plausibility to well-known classics of every age, not excepting our own, and produce similar results. This, in fact, has been done. The name of Richard Bentley, whose life ended a century and a half ago, is still held in the highest honour as one of the greatest scholars and critics that England has ever known. His success in disproving the authenticity of a series of letters which were ascribed to Phalaris, the semi-mythical tyrant of Sicily, seemed to invest him with a critical dictatorship. Queen Caroline is said to have expressed a wish that the great critic should exercise his talents upon an edition of Milton, and thus gratify those readers who could not enjoy his celebrated lucubrations on classical writers. 'Probably she thought (says Professor Jebb) that the learning, especially the classical learning, which enters so largely into Milton's epic would afford a good field for illustrative commentary to a classical scholar.' But the critic found what no one had hitherto suspected, that there were many words in the poem which Milton had never dictated, and not a few passages which were in no sense his. And of this strange phenomenon Bentley had a ready explanation to offer. The author was obnoxious to the government, poor, friendless, and, worst of all, blind, and 'could only dictate his verses to be writ by another.' The amanuensis made numerous mistakes in spelling and printing, which Bentley found no difficulty in correcting. But the *Editor* was the chief offender. 'The friend to whom Milton committed his copy, and the overseeing of the press, did so vilely execute the trust, that *Paradise* under his ignorance and audaciousness may be said to be *twice lost.*' This *Editor* is responsible for many careless changes of word or phrase, of which Bentley gives forty-eight examples. But that is not the worst. This Editor, knowing Milton's bad circumstances—the evil days and evil tongues—profited by them to perpetrate a deliberate fraud of the most heartless kind. Having a turn for verse-writing, he actually interpolated many lines of his own, of which Bentley's insight discovered 'sixty-six examples, which can be detected by their own silliness and unfitness.' Besides, Milton himself 'made some slips and inadvertencies.' 'There are some inconsistencies in the system and plan of his poem, for want of his revisal of the whole before its publication.' Sixteen examples of these are given. These are beyond merely verbal emendation, and require 'a change both of words and sense.'

It is quite unnecessary to criticize this criticism

of the great critic. The *Editor* who was guilty of
so much wrong owes his existence, as Professor Jebb
remarks, to Bentley's vigorous imagination. And if
any one should be curious to see what reply may be
made to the hypothetic charges of 'wilful interpola-
tions and inadvertent changes,' he will find it in the
professor's recent life of Bentley. Enough for my
purpose to exhibit Bentley's edition of *The Paradise
Lost* as a prophetic precursor of the editions of *The
Law of Moses, the Book of the Prophet Isaiah,* and
other portions of the Old Testament which are offered
to us by the Higher Critics ; only that the foreshadow-
ing was faint and timid. For whereas the critic of
Paradise Lost imagined only one Editor, the critics
of the Old Testament *imagine* many—a fresh one
whenever occasion renders it necessary—to whom,
under an appellation unknown to Old Testament
history, that of Redactor (? Reviser and Recon-
structor), is ascribed everything which the critic
thinks cannot have been original [1].

In maintaining that the ancient belief in the Mosaic
authorship of the Pentateuch is worthy of all accept-

---

[1] Dr. W. H. Green in his recent work, *The Higher Criticism
of the Pentateuch,* gives other modern illustrations of 'the pre-
carious character of the methods and results of subjective
criticism,' such as the 'systematic onset upon Cicero's orations
against Catiline, of whose genuineness there is abundant proof';
and a discussion which arose anent certain portions of Goethe's
Faust, which he sets forth as 'a beacon to warn classical philo-
logists against over-hasty interpolation-criticism.'—Pp. 127-130.

ation, and that the denial of it involves the destruction of confidence not merely in the inspiration of what we are accustomed to call Holy Scripture, but in its historic truthfulness, and in the veracity of its writers, we do not forget that an attempt is sometimes made to throw doubt on such conclusions by the off-hand averment that we have not the books of Moses as they came from the hands of Moses ; if indeed they were really his. This is a statement which is altogether misleading. We have these books substantially in the only form in which we have any evidence that they ever existed. To the remarks bearing on this point, which will be found in pp. 30–36, may be added an appeal to the Samaritan Pentateuch as a convincing witness to the integrity of ' The Law ' as it came from the hands of Moses. The Samaritans, whose national origin dates from the division of the kingdom on the death of Solomon, declined to accept the later books, which they identified with the rival kingdom of Judah. Had the books which are ascribed to Moses originated in the later age which the Higher Criticism imagines, they could not have become the Bible of the Samaritans.

There are one or two expressions and one or two verses which, it is affirmed, cannot have been written by Moses. Of these the words in Gen. xxxvi. 31 are specially insisted on : ' These are the kings that reigned in the land of Edom, before there reigned any king over the children of Israel.' These words, it is said, could not have been written till kingship was established in Israel. But Delitzsch holds that the narrator might have inserted this clause from the standpoint of the promise to Abraham in Gen. xvii. 6, and to Jacob in Gen. xxxv. 11.   And Dr. W. H. Green, recalling the fact that Edom had been a nation with dukes and kings for four hundred years, while Israel had been bondsmen and kingless all these centuries, it was only natural to mark the contrast, and after thorough discussion, concludes that ' instead of indicating an anachronism, the form of expression points directly to Moses as its author ' (*The Unity of the Book of Genesis*, pp. 425–429).

But even if this and a few other similar passages can be found which really point to a later age than that of Moses, it is not unreasonable to suppose that they were inserted by prophetic authority to make the story more intelligible to later readers.   Whereas if we ascribe the books themselves, as they now stand, to a later age we have to face all the difficulties—logical, historical, moral, and religious—which have been expounded within the too narrow limits of this Primer.

There is one chapter in the Book of Deuteronomy which it is certain that Moses did not write, that which contains the history of his death.   But the criticism which, because Moses did not write the account of his own death found in a book which bears his name, throws doubt on whether he did write, and suggests that he could not have written, the history of events and discourses found in the chapters which precede his death, scarcely deserves the trouble of refutation. It is almost like saying that because the dead man

could not tell us how he died, the living man could not
have told us how he lived, or what he did while he lived.

Instead of finding in the last chapter of Deuteronomy
any occasion of doubtfulness as to the Mosaic authorship of the Pentateuch, we find in it strongly corro-
borative evidence of the truth of the recorded history
of which it is the conclusion. For

(1) Why should the book—fivefold, as we have it,
but really one—be wound up with a detailed account
of the death, and that in very peculiar circumstances,
of the man Moses? The only answer that is at all
rational is—because of the extraordinary position which
this man had occupied, and the extraordinary work
which had been assigned to him, and whose faithfulness
in accomplishing it, as 'the servant of God,' the New
Testament does not shrink from comparing with the
faithfulness of Christ as 'the Son of God' (Heb. iii.
2 ; Numb. xii. 7).

And (2) why such a death? at once painful and
blessed—in one respect punitive, in another the reward
of faithful service? The preceding history, as we find
it in Numbers xx. 12 and xxvii. 12–14, explains its
double character. To Moses it must have been a priva-
tion of bitter severity to be deprived of the privilege
of leading the redeemed host into the promised land,
but at the same time it must have been a great joy to
see the land, and then to rest from his labours in the
peace of God.

Thus this last chapter of the Pentateuch would be
unintelligible without the history which certain critics

would stamp as untrustworthy, and that history would be incomplete without this record of the life's-end of the great leader and lawgiver, whose voice we hear and whose steps we follow through its pages. Who wrote this supplemental note we do not know. But how its incidents became known we can understand. As Elisha was permitted to accompany Elijah, and to talk with him, up to the moment when the chariot of fire separated them, so Joshua—why should we doubt it?—who had been honoured to attend on Moses as his minister on Horeb (Exod. xxiv. 13), was privileged to accompany Moses and hold converse with him until the Lord was pleased to separate them—it may be by a cloud—Moses to die, and Joshua to descend to his work as the Captain of Israel.

The verses which follow the account of the death of Moses, the last in the book, must have been written long after, probably centuries after, the events recorded in the book, but instead of suggesting doubt respecting the contents of the book, they confirm them. Why should we be told that 'no prophet like unto Moses whom the Lord knew face to face' had yet appeared in Israel? Because Moses was the Prophet of the book, and himself had foretold, as written in the book (ch. xviii.), that a prophet like unto him, endowed as he was, and divinely privileged as he was, should at some future time appear in Israel. The words with which the book closes put the seal of a later age on the prophecy and the book which contains it.

CONCLUSION

THERE are not a few questions which will occur to non-experts who read these pages, but I can do little more than refer to them. For example, How are we to regard the Bible as a whole in the light of the asserted results of the Higher Criticism? If these results in regard, say, to the Pentateuch and Joshua, to say nothing of Daniel and many separate passages and chapters in other histories and prophets, are genuine, and give us the truth respecting these Scriptures and portions of Scriptures, what effect will this have on our estimate of the Bible as a whole? I see no logical or common-sense answer to this question, but that the Bible must lose all credit for historical truthfulness or trustworthiness. I can understand the distinction which is insisted on when it is said that the Bible is not the Word of God, it is only the record of the Word—a distinction which is more apparent than real, for if it be a record of Divine revelations, such as is to be found in no other book or collection of books, neither in nature, which we are sometimes reminded is a word of God,

nor in Providence, which may claim the same honour,
—if it occupies so unique a position in the relations
between God and man, we cannot be far wrong in
calling it 'the Word of God.' It would be difficult
to dissuade the devout heart from using an appellation
which is not only convenient for its brevity, but which
puts emphasis on, and brings into prominence, the very
essence of the book.

But if it be a record of Divine revelations, we must
repudiate every theory and every shade of criticism
which would stamp any part as untruthful and untrustworthy. It is the voice of God Himself that
comes to us through Jeremiah, ' cursed be he that
doeth the work of the Lord deceitfully.' And further,
we need have no hesitation in applying to the critical
theory which we are discussing the words of Dean
Milman in regard to the once popular Tubingen
theory of the New Testament : ' It seems to me that
instead of the theory being the result of diligent and
acute investigation, the theory is first made, and then
the inferences or arguments sought out, discerned,
or imagined, and wrought up with infinite skill to
establish the foregone conclusion ; at the same time
with a contemptuous disregard or utter obtuseness
to the difficulties of their own system.'

At the same time out of evil God educeth good.
Whatever may be the immediate or ultimate effect
of the speculations of the Higher Criticism, we sym-
pathize entirely with the conclusion of Dr. William
Henry Green. 'While the hypothesis, i.e. of partition,

has proved futile as an attempt to account for the origin of the Pentateuch, the labour spent upon it has not been entirely thrown away, and it has not been without positive advantage to the cause of truth. (1) It has demonstrated the impossibility of such a partition. The experiment has been tried in every way that the utmost ingenuity could devise, but without success. (2) It has led to the development of a vast mass of positive evidence of unity, which would not otherwise have been so diligently sought for, and might not have been brought to light. (3) It has led to the elucidation and better understanding of the Pentateuch, from the necessity thus imposed of minute and thorough investigation of the meaning and bearings of every word and sentence, and of the mutual relations of every part. It verifies the old fable of a field which was dug over for a chimerical purpose, but the labour thus expended was rewarded, for an unlooked-for harvest sprung from seed which lay unsuspected in the soil' (*On the Higher Criticism of the Pentateuch*, p. 132).

I venture to add the words of warning in which Dr. Green concludes the volume from which I have just quoted. 'Within a very few years professedly evangelical men have ventured upon the hazardous experiment of attempting a compromise in this matter. They propose to accept these hypotheses in spite of their antibiblical character, in spite of their incompatibility with the historical truth of the Bible, in spite of their contravening its explicit statements.

in spite of the grave questions which they raise respecting the fallibility of our Lord's own teaching ; and they expect to retain their Christian faith with only such modifications as these newly adopted hypotheses may require.   They are now puzzling themselves over the problem of harmonizing Christ's sanction given to false views respecting the Old Testament with implicit faith in Him as a Divine Teacher.   And some of them in their perplexity over this enigma come perilously near impairing the truth of His claims.   Would it not be wiser for them to revise their own ill-judged alliance with the enemies of evangelical truth, and inquire whether Christ's view of the Old Testament may not, after all, be the true view ?'

In drawing this argument to a close the reader's attention is directed to the motto which appears on the title-page—'In understanding be men.'   The reader needs no help towards distinguishing between those attributes of childhood without which we cannot enter the Kingdom of Heaven, and those characteristics of which we are reminded by the words, 'that we henceforth be no more children tossed to and fro and carried about with every wind of doctrine.'   'Prove all things,' writes one apostle ; 'hold fast that which is good' (1 Thess. v. 21).   'Believe not every spirit,' says another, 'but try the spirits whether they are of God : because many false prophets are gone out into the world' (1 John iv. 1).   It is the author's hope that this little book will be subjected in all its reasonings

to the 'proving' and 'trying' which are thus enjoined
by apostolic authority.   It seeks no shelter for them
other than is found in their own validity and truth.
'In understanding be men.'

Children are subject to what may be called a centripetal and a centrifugal force. On the one hand they
are exposed to the danger of being drawn too strongly,
and of adhering too tenaciously to what they have
been taught, and what has become sacred through
early associations. And on the other hand they are
in danger of being drawn away too readily, startled or
frightened away, from what they have been taught by
bold and specious novelties, and the confidence, often
the supercilious confidence, of men who claim to have
discovered what has been hid from the ages that have
gone before. We have, as not children but men, on
the one hand to guard against a blind and obstinate
maintenance of inherited opinions in the face of reasons
that should suffice to quench them ; and equally to
guard against pretentious theories, whose chief power
or fascination is in their 'newness.' It cannot be too
strongly insisted upon, that while in science, and in
many of the practical applications of science, we have
to place ourselves in the hands of experts or specialists,
the materials for forming a judgement on the most
prominent religious problems of the day are within
the reach of ordinary intelligence, and ordinary intelligence has to guard against too facile yielding to either
centripetal or centrifugal forces.

Men are sometimes applauded for their courage in

breaking loose from old moorings, and advancing, as the phrase is, with the times. But it often requires more courage and more strength to hold fast by the old moorings than to break away from them. The times often advance the wrong way, and have to retrace their steps in search of light and truth. There is nothing more humiliating in the history of human thought than the record which it contains of bold conclusions, adopted in the very name of science, surrounded for a time with a glamour which makes it almost impious to question them, and then repudiated, cast away as vain idols—only, however, to give place to equally vain idols that may be worshipped for another season.   Dean Farrar, speaking of the critics which have from time to time assailed the authenticity of the Gospels, says, 'The schemes which have been proposed by rival critics with so much arrogant confidence and mutual contempt, have succeeded to each other in such bewildering multitudes, like waves rushing over waves, that we know not whether most to be astonished at their rapidity or to despise their evanescence[1].'   The remark is equally true of 'the schemes which have been proposed by critics' for revolutionizing our conceptions of the Old Testament, and reducing the avowed history of the ancient Church of God, very greatly into a mass of legends and myths, and, at the best, of well-intentioned endeavours of unknown men to do good by means which it would require a Jesuit's subtlety to distinguish from forgery.   Of these

[1] *Hulsean Lectures*, p. 52.

'schemes,' another dean, writing in very mild terms,
says in answer to the question, 'What does criticism
say?' 'Here it seems to me that while the questions
have been innumerable, and the answers also, the
crop of clear, certain, and convincing answers, has
been a singularly small one. Nothing seems to me
more remarkable than the contrast in our time between
the certainties of physical science, and the contradictory and uncertain results, the barrenness, as a
whole, of criticism applied to the questions which
most interest men [1].'

Had Dean Farrar carried to the study of the Book
of Daniel the principles which he maintained so
eloquently in his Hulsean Lectures in defence of the
Gospels, he would not have accepted the conclusions
of the extremest Rationalism, conclusions which, if
true, should drive the book ignominiously out of the
canon of Holy Scripture. He would have found no
difficulty in proving—and this has often been done—
that the Daniel of the Book was what Christ called
him, a 'Prophet,' and one who was honoured to supply
Christ Himself with words in which to describe the
glory of His second coming (Matt. xxvi. 64).

The late learned Dr. Cairns, writing to his friend
Dr. John Brown, said, 'The dulness of criticism [of
the Rationalist school] is seen in the non-appreciation
of the grandeur of Daniel, which every fool of the
Maccabean age is supposed capable of having written,
or according to some, a joint-stock company or for-

[1] *Life of Dean Church*, p. 337.

tuitous concourse of fools and fanatics, whose fabrications run into such sublime shapes as Belshazzar's vision, and Daniel's prayer, not to speak of Nebuchadnezzar's dream. Surely the time will come in all lands when some sort of elementary feeling for the sacred and the great will be so diffused as to nip such absurdities in the bud, and serve as a foundation for the positive Scripture criticism and exposition to build upon [1].'

The unlearned non-experts, whose rights and powers we here plead, need have no fear for the future of their Bible. They need no aid from superstition or ignorance to defend the Book, nor need they shut their eyes against any light that may come from true criticism, from historical discovery, from linguistic progress, or from profounder insight into the truths of revelation. Its destined course among the nations is that of the 'Light, which shineth more and more unto the perfect day.'

[1] *Life of Dr. Cairns*, p. 432.

www.ingramcontent.com/pod-product-compliance
Lightning Source LLC
Chambersburg PA
CBHW032245080426
42735CB00008B/1016